PURITAN PAPERBACKS

Gospel Life

John Owen

1616–1683

John Owen was born in 1616 in Stadhampton, Oxford-shire and died in Ealing, West London, in 1683. During his sixty-seven years he lived out a life full of spiritual experience, literary accomplishment, and national influence so beyond most of his peers that he continues to merit the accolade of 'the greatest British theologian of all time.' Despite his other achievements, Owen is best famed for his writings. They are characterized by profundity, thoroughness and, consequently, authority. Although many of his works were called forth by the particular needs of his own day, they all have a uniform quality of timelessness.

John Owen

Gospel Life

THE BANNER OF TRUTH TRUST

THE BANNER OF TRUTH TRUST

Head Office
3 Murrayfield Road
Edinburgh, EH12 6EL
UK

North America Office
610 Alexander Spring Road
Carlisle, PA 17015
USA

banneroftruth.org

The sermons in this volume have been selected from
The Works of John Owen, volume 9
This modernized edition © The Banner of Truth Trust 2023
First published 2023

ISBN
Print: 978 1 80040 326 0
Epub: 978 1 80040 327 7
Kindle: 978 1 80040 328 4

*

Typeset in 10/13 Minion Pro at
The Banner of Truth Trust, Edinburgh

Printed in Poland
by Arka, Cieszyn

Unless otherwise stated, all Scriptural quotations are taken
from THE HOLY BIBLE, English Standard Version,
© Copyright 2001 by Crossway Bibles,
a division of Good News Publishers.
Used by permission. All rights reserved.

Footnotes from the William H. Goold edition of 1850–53 have
been retained. New footnotes have also been added and the text
has been modernized.

The Trust wishes to express its gratitude to
Dr John Aaron for his assistance in
the production of this volume.

Contents

Publisher's Introduction

JOHN OWEN pastored the Independent congregation at Leadenhall Street, London, from 1673 until his death in 1683. Many of the sermons preached during this period were taken down in short-hand by Sir John Hartopp, a member of the congregation, who then transcribed them fully in long-hand. After Owen's death a number of the sermons were published, some in 1721 and others in 1756. They were all eventually included in Volume 9 of William H. Goold's 1850–53 edition of Owen's *Works*.[1]

Of the forty-three sermons contained in these two tranches of posthumous sermons, the thirteen included in this book are connected by the same general theme. In each of them Owen takes up some aspect of the experience of a Christian; aspects of *Gospel Life*. The sermons were preached within a period of about thirteen years and are a product of Owen's most mature views as a theologian and pastor. The spiritual graces dealt with are those of *saving faith, love, humility, persevering faith* and *hope*.

In the first two sermons, Owen is dealing with saving faith: the faith in Christ that justifies us before God. He begins by describing the nature of this faith:

[1] John Owen, *Works*, Vol. 9 (London: Banner of Truth Trust, 1965).

> Someone who has the least faith has as true a share, though not so clear a share, in the righteousness of Christ as the most steadfast believer. Others may be more holy than he, but no one in the world is more righteous than he. His sanctification will inevitably be shallow, for little faith will produce only little obedience; if the root is weak, the fruit will not be great. But he is second to none in justification (pp. 17-18).

He then proceeds with his main purpose in the sermons, that of encouraging believers to maintain the strength of their faith: their 'steadfastness in the promises.' Maintaining a steadfast faith is the pre-eminent way of bringing glory to God.

The third sermon (sermon 3) was preached on 5 June, 1673, the day that John Owen's small, Independent congregation that he had gathered together in London (amounting to some thirty-six members) united with the nearby Independent congregation meeting at Leadenhall Street. This was a much larger group of one hundred and thirty-six members that had been pastored by the well-known Puritan commentator, Joseph Caryl, until his death some four months earlier. At a time when many adjustments and changes were almost certainly having to be made, the new pastor, speaking for the first time to his new congregation, chose to address them on 'love, which binds everything together in perfect harmony.'

> Let no one then pretend that they love their brothers and sisters, in general, and love the people of God, and love the saints, while their love is not fervently exercised towards those who are in the same church society as themselves. Christ has given it to you as a test; he will

try your love at the last day according to your behaviour in the church of which you are a member (p. 70).

The five sermons on humility (sermons 4 to 8) show Owen concentrating on what he sees as the essence of humility, namely, 'a humble walking before God.' He notes the need for agreement, for unity and for life, if two are to walk together, and then describes in detail the necessary submission to the rule of God's grace and the rule of his providence if we are to walk humbly. Thus, for example:

Man sees and knows his own righteousness and walk with God. He sees what it costs him, and where it places him. He knows what pains he has taken to obtain it; what waiting, fasting, labouring and praying it has cost him. He knows how he has deprived himself of his natural desires and mortified his flesh in abstaining from sin. These are the things of a man, wrought in him, performed by him; and the spirit of a man knows them. These provide a fair promise to the man who has been sincere in them, for whatever goal or purpose he would use them. But as for the righteousness of Christ, that is outside of himself, he does not see it, nor has experienced it. The spirit which is within him knows nothing of it. He has no acquaintance with it except as it is revealed and offered in the promises. And these even, do not tell him that this righteousness is his – provided for him in particular – but only that it is promised to and provided for believers. Now, for a man to throw away that which he can see in order to obtain what he cannot see; to refuse that which promises to supply him with some support and good hope in God's presence, and which he knows belongs to him and cannot be taken away from him, to throw it away for something which

> he must take by faith, based upon the word of a promise, and in spite of ten thousand doubts, fears and temptations that it does not in fact belong to him: such a step requires the soul to be humbled before God, something which a man's heart is not easily brought to (pp. 125-126).

He concludes by showing that walking humbly before God is both our greatest duty and our most precious concern.

In the next two sermons (sermons 9 and 10), Owen returns to the theme of faith. These were preached on 11 November and 25 November, 1670, respectively. In this case, however, he deals not with saving faith specifically, as in sermons 1 and 2, but with persevering faith: that faith which maintains a believer through all the troubles and oppressions that are met with in the Christian life. In overwhelming circumstances what supports our faith, and provides relief through faith, is our knowledge of the nature of God himself in all his attributes; in particular, the knowledge of the sovereignty of his grace:

> There is another great argument, when all is brought to the sovereignty of God's will, found in Romans 8:32. 'He who did not spare his own Son but gave him up for us all, how will he not also with him graciously give us all things?' Shall I question whether or not God will answer this prayer or the other, when I consider this great example of his will? It was his will to send Jesus Christ to die for poor sinners. He did not send him to die in vain, and that his death should be lost. If God is not willing to dispense grace and mercy to sinners, why did he send Jesus Christ? Why did he give up his own Son out of his bosom? Why did he not spare him and leave our iniquities to meet upon us? Can God give a greater sign of his readiness to spare sinners

than the way in which he dealt with Jesus Christ? (pp. 200-201).

Finally (in sermons 11, 12 and 13), he turns to the subject of hope. These sermons were preached on 26 September, 3 October, and 10 October, 1680. Believers must always be ready to witness to their hope of the physical resurrection and of eternal life. As he proceeds through these sermons, Owen shows again the centrality of faith in a believer's life. The strength of our hope is very dependent on the strength of our faith. It is faith that enables the believer not to be taken by surprise by death, and faith that commits the soul to God's care at death.

> As to how this duty is carried out, it ought to be done in words expressed directly to God. I am not instructing those who are dying, but you who live, in order that you should be prepared to die. You should say to God, 'Lord, I have been this long in the world; I have seen much variety in the outward disposal of things, but a thousand times more variety in the inward frame of my spirit. I am now leaving the world at your call. I am to be no more. O Lord, all being over, being about to enter a new, eternal state, I commit my soul to you – I leave it with you – I put all my trust and confidence in your faithfulness, power and sovereignty, to be dealt with according to the terms of the covenant of grace. Now I can lie down in peace' (pp. 221-222).

Throughout these sermons, Owen shows that in every aspect of gospel life 'the righteous shall live – and die – by faith.'

Gospel Ministry, a companion volume to *Gospel Life*, is also available. It is made up of nine sermons by John Owen on aspects of Christian ministry, all of which are also taken from Volume 9 of his works and adapted into modernized English.

Sermon 1

The Strength of Faith[1]

No distrust made him waver concerning the promise of God,
but he grew strong in his faith as he gave glory to God.
—Rom. 4:20

In this chapter the apostle singles out a specific example in order to demonstrate the conclusion which, by many convincing arguments, he had proved in the previous chapter; namely, that the justification of a sinner cannot be brought about or accomplished except by the righteousness of faith in Christ. He does so by describing, from the beginning of the chapter to the end of verse 17, the example of Abraham, the testimonies given concerning him and the way by which he was justified before God. From verse 18 to the end of verse 22 he describes that faith of Abraham, by which he obtained acceptance with God, so that he might present him as an example and encouragement to us all.

Among the excellent characteristics of this faith, seen in its cause, object, content and manner, which I shall not now

---

[1] Owen notes that this sermon was preached a considerable time ('long since') after another sermon on the same text preached before Parliament in February 1649 or 1650 (see note by W. H. Goold in *Works,* vol. 8, p. 208).

comment on, not the least is stated in my text: 'No distrust made him waver concerning the promise of God.'

There is a *meiosis* [*litotes*] in these words, an expression of an affirmative by strongly negating its opposite: 'No distrust made him waver'; that is, he was steadfast in believing, or, as it is explained at the end of the verse, 'he grew strong in faith.'

These words provide us with two observations:

Observation 1: *All distrust is through lack of faith.*

The apostle says, 'No distrust made him waver.' Men are prone to provide many other reasons and to blame various obstacles but, in reality, all our wavering is through unbelief. But I have some time ago, in a different way, demonstrated, proved and applied this truth (see footnote 1 above).

There is another proposition in the text to which I shall now turn.

Observation 2: *Steadfastness in believing the promises is greatly acceptable to God.*

In dealing with this subject, I shall do two things: 1. Explain the terms of the proposition; 2. Confirm the truth of it.

I. *The explanation of this proposition*

1. *The object with which it is dealing is 'the promises': the promises of God.* These are the declarations of the purposes of God's grace towards his elect, according to the tenor of the covenant. What is being referred to in the text is the great promise of old to Christ, which contains all other promises within it; that 'all the promises of God find their Yes in him' (2 Cor. 1:20). So that although I shall not say

anything which is not true with respect to every promise of God, yet my main regard will be to those promises that exhibit Christ and the free grace of God in him to sinners, and to steadfastness in believing these promises.

2. *The action exercised with respect to this object; namely, believing.* It is firmness in believing that we are considering.

I shall not spend much time on the nature of faith nor on detailing the different views held among men of it, but only mention what is needed for us to agree on what is being described.

The great number of disputes there have been among men on the nature of faith – the subject, its proper object, the formal reason for it – are familiar to you. And those who have carefully studied these matters will soon realize how little the church of God owes to men who have made it their concern to press upon all believers these intricate disputes as to general duties and absolute necessities. By some men's too much understanding, others have been brought to understand nothing at all. Anyone who wishes to have his own spiritual experience and daily duty made unintelligible to him, let him consider these philosophical disputes. Some place faith in one distinct category of the soul, some in another, and some say that there are no such things as distinct categories of the soul. Some place it in both the two chief aspects of the soul: the will and the understanding; others say that it is impossible that one attribute should reside in two faculties.

For my part, my main intention is to speak to those whom God chooses: the poor and foolish of the world. The means by which he will bring these to himself will, I am sure, not be above the understanding which he has given them (1 John 5:20). Although the usual way, by most, when expounding faith is to use strict terms so that it may be presented with philosophical exactness, yet, consistently, the method used by the Holy Spirit to teach it is by metaphorical expressions, accommodating it to things of sense and common daily use, giving an enjoyment and perception of it to all who have an interest. This is how I shall attempt to speak, so that everyone who does believe may also know what is involved in believing.

But note this, particularly: I will be speaking of believing and of faith only with reference to their end and purpose discussed here by Paul; that is, with respect to justification by faith and our acceptance with God.

(i) *Faith, or believing, in this limited sense does not consist solely in the assent of the mind to the truth of the promises, or of any one promise.* When someone tells us something, and we say we believe him – that is, that we believe what he has said is true – then there is this assent of the mind. Without this there is no faith. But this alone is not the faith that we are talking about. This, on its own, the devils have, and cannot choose not to have (James 2:19). They believe that which makes them shudder, doing so on the authority of God who reveals it.

You might answer, 'The devil believes only the threats of God: that which makes him tremble. His belief therefore is not a general assent but a partial one. It is different from our belief, which is a faith in everything that God has revealed, especially the promises.'

I would answer that the devil believes the promises as much as he does the threats of God; that is, that they are true and shall be fulfilled. It is part of his misery that he has to believe them. And the promises of God make him tremble just as much as God's threats do. The first promise to us was given in the context of a threat to him (Gen. 3:15). And there is no promise in which there is not a threat to him involved. Every word concerning Christ, or grace by Christ, speaks of his downfall and ruin. Indeed, his destruction lies more in the promises than in the threats. Promises are what weaken him daily and give him a continual foretaste of his approaching destruction.

With this in mind it is clear that believing, or faith, cannot only be an assent to the truths of those promises, based on the fidelity of the one who promises. This is its foundation and is why it is called 'the receiving the testimony of God' in which we set our seal that God is true (John 3:33). Yet, I think that there is more again to receiving the testimony of God and setting our seal to it (agreeing, as when making a contract, that it is so and will remain so) than the bare assent of the mind to the truth of the promises. In everyday speech, to receive a man's testimony means no more than believing what he says is true, but in the expression 'setting our seal,' there seems to be included that which God speaks of to Job, 'Hear, and know it for your good' (Job 5:27). There is a receiving for ourselves included in these expressions, which involves much more than bare assent. I would say then that this assent is of faith, though it is not faith. And in saying that it is not justifying faith, I am not denying it, but affirming it be of the nature of faith in general. The addition of a specific assent does not destroy the nature of anything. Faith in general therefore is this kind of assent which has been described.

(ii) *Nor is it the assent of the will alone that is involved in receiving the promise as something good and suitable.* The content of the promise must be considered when believing, as well as the promise itself. Christ, with his righteousness and benefits, is, as it were, offered to us in it. Therefore, when we believe, we are said to accept, to 'receive reconciliation' ('receive the atonement,' KJV) (Rom. 5:11). To agree that the content of the promise (that which is presented in its words) is good and desirable, that is, good and desirable to us, and to choose it on that account, is also, therefore, a necessary part of believing. It is what is meant by 'receiving Christ' (John 1:12). But it is not exactly and exclusively this. Sarah's faith is described as: 'she considered him faithful who had promised' (Heb. 11:11). And this is of the nature of faith, as I mentioned before, the considering, or judging, him faithful who had promised, and assenting to the truth of his promises on that account. Now, the first of these may be without the second: our assenting may occur without the accompanying choosing of the will; but the latter cannot occur without the former. There is an assenting which certainly involves a choosing also.

(iii) *I suppose I need not now add that believing does not entirely consist in acceptance by the affections, and the embracing by them of the things promised.* The stony ground received the word immediately (Matt. 13:20). It is said (verse 5) that the seed sprang up immediately because they had no depth of soil. When men have warm hearts but not thoroughly prepared minds and hearts, they may immediately take up the word and express great things about it; but where it is sown deeply it is usually longer before it appears.

[6]

When a man receives the word only in the affections, the first touch of them cannot be hidden. He will speak of it instantly, melt under it, and declare how he has been affected by it: 'Oh, this sermon has done me much good!' But this is not faith when it is on its own. They receive the word with joy but have no root in themselves (verses 20, 21). When Christ promised 'the bread of life,' that is, himself, how many were immediately affected and expressed strong desires for it! 'Sir,' they said, 'give us this bread always' (John 6:34). They liked it, they desired it immediately, their affections were taken with it. And yet they were only 'temporary,' not true believers, for after a while they 'turned back and no longer walked with him' (verse 66). Wouldn't you expect that those 'who have tasted the heavenly gift' (Heb. 6:4) would like the taste, and be affected by it? There are, indeed, many who deceive in this situation. I could give examples of very many who have been affected by the word of promise, preached or considered, but have done so for so many false and unsound reasons, so many sandy foundations, that we cannot at all conclude that to believe is entirely a matter of the affections. When affections go before believing, they are of very little worth; but when they follow it they are very acceptable and precious in God's sight.

(iv) *Neither is believing merely 'fiducia': a trust, reliance or confidence.* There is a twofold fiducial trust. Firstly, one by which we trust in Christ *for* the forgiveness of sin: which we might call adherence. It is an adhering to Christ in that we trust in him for the forgiveness of sins and acceptance with God. To the degree that we trust, to that degree we cling to him, but no more. There is secondly a trust that our sins *are* forgiven; we trust, or rest, upon it. Now, neither of these can be faith in its entirety, so that the whole of faith should be included in them. There is something more in believing than in trusting; and something more in trusting than is absolutely necessary to include the entire notion of believing, for we may believe something in which we do not have complete assurance. But I grant this, that where you have belief in Christ, you have a trust in him, to some degree or other. And when faith is increased to a good height, strength and firmness, it predominantly involves trust and confidence (John 14:1). To believe in such a way as to free our hearts from trouble and fear of whatever kind, is therefore to trust fully. Doubting, wavering and fearing, which in Scripture are condemned as being opposed to faith, are indeed directly opposite to this fiduciary resting our souls on Christ. This is how the apostle describes his faith (2 Tim. 1:12). To believe so as to be convinced that God is able to guard what we commit to him, is to put our trust in him.

(v) Having said as much about these four aspects, without touching on all the arbitrary definitions of the schools, and the exactness of words of various philosophical rules and terms, I shall give a general description of faith or believing that answers, in some measure, the proper, illustrative expressions of it in the Scriptures, where it is termed: *looking or seeing, hearing, tasting, resting, rolling ourselves, flying for refuge, trusting,* and similar phrases.

(a) There must be, what I spoke of first of all, *an assent of the mind* to the whole truth of the promises of God based on this foundation, that he is able and faithful to accomplish them. This is certainly involved in, though it is not all of, our *receiving the testimony*, or witness, of God (John 3:33). Sarah, previously mentioned, received the testimony of God. How did she do so? She 'considered him faithful who had promised' (Heb. 11:11). God presents this to us, in the first place. Eternal life is promised by God, 'who never lies' (Titus 1:2); that is, who is so faithful that it is utterly impossible that he should deceive anyone. 'So when God desired to show more convincingly to the heirs of the promise the unchangeable character of his purpose, he guaranteed it with an oath, so that by two unchangeable things, in which it is impossible for God to lie, we who have fled for refuge might have strong encouragement to hold fast to the hope set before us' (Heb. 6:17, 18). God's purpose is that we should receive encouragement as we fly for refuge to lay hold of the hope set before us; that is, by believing. What does he offer for our encouragement? Why, his own faithfulness and immutability founded on the promise of his word and upon his oath. This also was the nature of Abraham's faith, as described and commended in Romans 5.

The Scriptures mention various attributes of God on the basis of which, if I might put it that way, our souls are to assent to the truth of his promises and to accept them. Two are mentioned particularly:

First, his *power*: 'He is able' (Rom. 4:21; 11:23).

Secondly, his *faithfulness*: as in the references already mentioned, and many others.

The sum is that, on the basis of God's faithfulness and power, this is what we must do if we are to believe: we are to assent to the truth of his promises and to the certainty of their fulfilment. If this is not done it is in vain to go forward. Let those, then, who hope to gain some advantage from what is to be mentioned later, stop here a little, and judge how well they have laid this foundation. There are many who have never been able to arrive at any stability throughout their days and have never discerned the reason for their wavering and unsteadiness. In fact, their foundation was not laid in an orderly manner. This first acceptance of the faithfulness and power of God in the promises was never distinctly comprehended and acted upon by their souls. And if the foundation is weak, no matter how glorious the building, it will totter, or even fall. Look back then to the beginning of your faith, to ensure that it is not failing you. Then, when every other support is failing, this will keep you from sinking.

(b) Over and above this first aspect, faith is expressed in Scripture (and we find it the case in our experience) as *the consent and acceptance of the will* to the Lord Jesus Christ as mediator. We accept him, having accomplished his work, as the only way of going to the Father, as the sole and sufficient cause of our acceptance with him, as our only righteousness before him.

It has been said that faith is the receiving of Christ as a priest and as a lord; to be saved by him and to be ruled by him. This sounds very well. Who is so wicked that, in endeavouring to believe, is not willing to be ruled by Christ as well as being saved by him? A faith that would not have Christ to be Lord over us is that faith which James rejects. He who wishes to be saved by Christ but not ruled by him, will not be saved by him at all. We are to receive a whole Christ, not by halves; receive him with respect to all his offices, not one or another.

It sounds well and looks good; indeed, in some respect, there is truth in it. But *latet anguis in herba*.[2] If men explained fully what was meant, it would be this: 'The receiving of Christ as a king is the yielding of obedience to him. But this subjection is not a fruit of the faith by which we are justified, but an essential part of it. There is no difference between faith and works, or obedience, in the matter of justification; both equally are a condition of it.'

When I read recently of someone saying, 'That this was one principle that the Church of England was based on, in the Reformation, that faith and works have the same significance in the business of justification,' I could only stand amazed and conclude that either he or I had been asleep ever since we were born; or that there were two Churches of England – one that I never knew, and another that he never knew – or else that prejudice is very powerful and makes men confident. Is that truly the doctrine of the Church of England, as they call it? When, where, and by whom in England was this taught, other than by Papists and Socinians, until within a very few years ago? What place does it have in the confessions, liturgies, polemical writers, or anyone else of any reputation for learning and religion in England? But this is not the place or time for disputing.

Others write at length, mincing matters, and saying that faith and works have the same significance only with respect to that justification that shall be made public and solemn at the last day, the day of judgment. Is this really all that they intended? How they will then justify themselves

---

[2] 'The snake lurks in the grass.'

at the day of judgment for troubling the peace of the saints of God and shaking the great fundamental articles of the Reformation, I do not know. But it is nothing new for men who love novelties to argue themselves into some unanticipated corner, and then to withdraw or retire with little grace.

We acknowledge then that faith receives Christ as a lord, as a king. Any faith that will not, or does not, do so – that will not submit the soul to all that obedience which he, as the captain of our salvation, requires from us – is not a true faith. But faith, as justifying faith, engages with Christ (in its varying degrees and nature of assent, as discussed) only for righteousness and acceptance with God. And, if you will allow me to say, in that act it excludes good works just as much as it excludes sin. It deals with Christ for that by which he is our righteousness and by which we are justified.

But you will say, 'This makes you Solifidians![3] Isn't this true of you?'

I say, Paul also was a Solifidian, whose epistles will prove all the formalists and self-justifiers in the world to be false. We are Solifidians with respect to justification: Christ, grace and faith are all. We are not Solifidians with respect to salvation and gospel living, nor in the demonstration of the efficacy of our faith. All the apostles of Christ, who excluded everything as a factor in our justification other than our acceptance by the grace of God once our faith had received Christ for righteousness, were such Solifidians. But all so-called Solifidians who exclude or deny the necessity of works and gospel obedience by those who are justified,

[3] A name derived from two Latin words, signifying *faith alone*.—W. H. Goold.

or who say that a true, justifying faith may exist without holiness, works and obedience, are condemned by all the apostles, and by James in particular.

This, then, is what is required in faith, or believing: that we receive Christ; 'His own people did not receive him' (John 1:11). Not receiving Christ for the purposes which the Father sent him to us, is true unbelief. It follows, therefore, that receiving him is true faith, or believing (verse 12). In preaching the gospel, we are therefore said to offer and present Christ, just as the Scriptures do (Rev. 22:17). The answer to an offer or an invitation is its acceptance. So that the soul's willing acceptance of the Lord Jesus Christ for our righteousness, offered to us in the promises of the gospel, for that end and purpose, from the love of the Father, is the core of that believing which is so acceptable to God.

(c) Add to this that which I cannot say is absolutely of the nature of faith, but is, to some degree or other (secret, or known to the soul), a necessary element of faith; namely, *the soul's resting and establishing itself, and satisfying its affections in its interest in, and enjoyment of, a sweet, desirable Saviour.* It is called 'clinging ('cleaving,' KJV) to the Lord' (Josh. 23:8): the fixing and fastening of our affections on God, as ours in covenant. The soul rests in God, trusting and confiding in him.

In these three things, which are understandable to the poorest soul and written clearly in the words of Scripture and in the experiences of those who deal with God in Christ, do I recognize the elements of that believing which is so acceptable to God.

3. *We next consider how this believing is qualified, as expressed in our original proposition.* It was believed firmly, steadfastly. This was expressed in the negative. Abraham's faith did not waver. To explain this, consider the following observations:

(i) Faith, or believing, consists in a frame of heart and actions of the soul that are capable of degrees of expansion and contraction, of strength and weakness. There is there-fore mention in Scripture of great faith: 'O woman, great is your faith,' and of weak faith, 'O you of little faith.' There is strong faith, as Abraham was 'strong in his faith,' and of being weak in faith, 'Receive him who is weak in the faith.' There is a faith which includes doubting, 'O you of little faith, why do you doubt?' and a faith that has no doubt, 'No distrust made him waver … but he grew strong in his faith.'

(ii) Every degree of faith is of equal sincerity, in every regard. They are equal with respect to all the main effects and advances of faith: in justification, in perseverance and in salvation. A little faith is not less a faith than a great faith; indeed, a little faith will carry a man as safely to heaven as a great faith, though not so comfortably or fruitfully.

(iii) Steadfastness has respect to these different degrees of faith. It is not of the nature of faith, but is that degree of faith which it pleases God that we should have and is in every way advantageous to ourselves. It is mentioned by Peter – 'Take care that you are not carried away … and lose your own stability' (2 Pet. 3:17), declining from that stability of faith which you had attained – and also by Paul (Col. 2:5).

(iv) There may therefore be a true faith which has many troublesome, perplexing doubts accompanying it, much sinful wavering attending it, without it being overthrown. It continues as a true faith still. Men may be true believers and yet not strong believers. A child who exists on milk has as true a human nature as a grown-up man who eats meat. Steadfastness refers to stability of faith with respect to the three elements previously mentioned, and by it a faith is made strong and effectual. It involves:

(a) A well-founded, firm, unshaken assent to the truth of the promises. It is therefore opposed to all doubting (James 1:5, 6).

(b) A resolved, clear consent to seek and receive Christ for life, as offered in the promise. This also is opposed to all troublesome, unsettling, perplexing doubts.

(c) The settled satisfaction of the soul upon the choice made and a warm consenting to it. This again opposes all abiding troubles (John 14:1).

This steadfastness in believing does not exclude all external temptations. When we say a tree is firmly rooted that does not mean that the wind never blows upon it. The house that is built on the rock is not free from assaults and storms. The captain of our salvation, the founder and perfecter of our faith, was tempted, and we shall be also if we follow him. Nor does it exclude all doubting from within. So long as we are in the flesh, though our faith be steadfast, we shall have unbelief, and that bitter root will produce more, or less, fruit according to the opportunities Satan gets to water it. But it does exclude falling under that temptation, with all the trouble and distresses that result: the abiding perplexing doubts which make us stagger to and fro between hope and fear; questioning whether we have truly believed in Christ or not, whether we have any real interest in the promise or not; the accompanying spiritual unhappiness and sadness, with real uncertainty as to the outcome.

This, then is what I mean by *steadfastness in believing*: the establishing of our hearts on receiving Christ offered by the love of the Father, to the peace and stability of our souls and consciences. That our hearts should be fixed, settled and established in this way – that we should live in the sense and power of it – is, I say, greatly acceptable to God.

There is a twofold evil and miscarriage among us in this great business of establishing our coming to Christ in the promise. Some spend all their days in much darkness and sadness, arguing to and fro in their own minds whether they have a true interest in the promise, or not. They are off and on, living and dying, hoping and fearing; and, usually, fearing most when they have the strongest hold: this is the nature of doubting. When they are completely cast down then they set themselves to labour for a recovery, and when they have regained a comforting assurance they instantly fear that all is not well and right, that things are not as they should be. And so they stagger to and fro all their lives, to the grief of the Spirit of God, and the discomfort of their own souls.

Others, beginning with a serious intent of coming to Christ on true terms, find it a difficult work, tedious to flesh and blood. They relapse into generalities, discontinue their seeking, and take it for granted that no more can be done. In this way they grow formal and complacent.

To help avoid both these evils, I shall confirm the proposition I stated at the beginning, but before doing so I wish to note some corollaries that follow from what has been said so far.

Corollary 1: Though a little weak faith, where steadfastness is lacking, will carry a man to heaven, yet it will never carry him there comfortably or pleasantly.

Someone whose faith is weak will have to pass through many desperate circumstances. Every blast of temptation will disturb his comfort, even if it does not turn him aside from obedience. At best, he is like a man who is bound by a chain on top of a high tower; though he cannot fall, he cannot stop being frightened. However, all will end well.

Corollary 2: The least true faith will do its work safely, though not so sweetly.

The smallest degree of faith gives the soul a share in the first resurrection. It is that principle of life which we receive when we are first quickened. However weak our life shall be, it is still a life that will never fail. It is of the seed of God which abides; incorruptible seed, which does not die. A believer is spirit, quickened from the dead. However young he may be, however sick, however weak, he is still alive, and the second death will have no power over him. A little faith provides a whole Christ. Someone who has the least faith has as true a share, though not so clear a share, in the righteousness of Christ as the most steadfast believer. Others may be more holy than he, but no one in the world is more righteous than he. His sanctification will inevitably be shallow, for little faith will produce only little obedience; if the root is weak, the fruit will not be great. But he is second to none in justification. The most imperfect faith will give present justification because it gives the soul a share in a present Christ. The lowest degree of true faith gives the highest completeness of righteousness (Col. 2:10). You who have only a weak faith yet have a strong Christ. Though all the world should set itself against your weak faith, it would not prevail. Sin cannot prevail, Satan cannot, hell cannot. Though you have taken only a weak, faint hold of Christ, he has taken a sure, strong and unconquerable hold of you. Haven't you often wondered how this spark of heaven could be kept alive in the middle of the sea? It is because it is everlasting, a spark that cannot be quenched, a drop of that fountain that can never wholly be dried up. Jesus Christ takes special care of those who are weak in faith (Isa. 40:11). For whatever reason they are sick and weak and disabled, this good Shepherd takes care of them. 'He shall stand … and they shall dwell secure' (Mic. 5:4).

Corollary 3: There may be faith, a little faith, where there is no steadfastness and much doubting.

Firmness and steadfastness are eminent qualifications which not all achieve, so there may be faith where there is doubting, though I am not saying that there must be. Doubts, in themselves, are opposed to believing. They are, if I can put it this way, unbelieving. A man can hardly believe all his life without some doubts, but a man may doubt all his days and never believe. If I see a field overgrown with thistles and weeds, I can say, 'There may be corn there, but still the weeds and thistles are not corn.' I say this, because some have no better foundation for their peace than that they have lacked peace, that they have doubted. Doubting may exist alongside belief, but we cannot conclude that where there is doubting there is faith; doubts may arise against presumption and complacency as well as against believing. But notice that there are two kinds of doubting:

(i) Doubts concerning the end. Men question what will become of them at the end; they fluctuate in their thoughts with regard to their last end. Balaam did so when he cried: 'Let me die the death of the upright, and let my end be like his' (Num. 23:10). That wretched man was tossed up and down between hopes and fears. This is common to the vilest person in the world. It is just the shaking of their security when they are alone.

(ii) Doubts about the means. The soul doubts whether it loves Christ, and whether Christ loves it or not. This is far more genuine than the first. It shows, at least, that such a soul is convinced of the excellence and worth of Christ, and that it values him. Indeed, this may sometimes be due to jealousy arising from fervour of love and not from weakness of faith. But with these doubts, faith, at least a little faith, may co-exist. This was the case of the poor man who cried out, 'I believe; help my unbelief!' (Mark 9:24). There is believing and unbelieving, faith and doubting, both at work at the same time in the same person: Jacob and Esau struggling in the same womb.

Application

Men who doubt should not conclude that they believe. He who is sure that his field has corn because it has thistles, may come short of a harvest. If your fears are more about the end than the means – more about future happiness than present communion with God – you can scarcely have a clearer proof of a false, corrupt frame of heart. Some flatter themselves with this, that they have doubted and trembled; but now they thank God they are quiet and at rest. How they came to be so, they can hardly tell: only that whereas they were once disturbed and troubled, and now all is well with them. I have known many like this, who, while under conviction, had many perplexing thoughts about their state and condition, but after a while, their convictions have worn off, the doubts which it produced have departed, and they have sunk down into a cold, lifeless frame. This is a miserable state of quiet. If the only way of casting out doubts and fears was by believing, all might be well; but presumption and complacency will do it also, at least for a season.

I mention these things only in passing, with reference to what was said previously.

II. *I now proceed to confirm the proposition laid down: Steadfastness in believing the promises is greatly acceptable to God, in accordance with the explanation I have provided.*

1. *I shall do this firstly from Scripture.*

(i) Consider the text itself: 'He grew strong in his faith as he gave glory to God.' All that God requires in any man or woman is his glory; that which he will not give to any other (Isa. 42:8). Let God have his glory and we may take freely whatever we wish: take Christ, take grace, take heaven, take all. The great glory which he will give to us consists in our giving him his glory and beholding it. Now if this is the great thing, the only thing that God requires of us – if this is the sum of that which he has reserved for himself, that he should be glorified as God, as our God – then anyone who gives him that, gives him what is acceptable to him. In this way Abraham pleased God by being strong and steadfast in believing. He grew strong in faith as he gave glory to God.

The glory of God is spoken of in various senses in Scripture:

(a) The Hebrew word for 'glory' signifies '*pondus*' or 'weight'; the apostle refers to it when he speaks of 'an eternal weight of glory' (2 Cor. 4:17). This is the glory of the thing itself. It also signifies splendour or brightness, as when the apostle writes of 'the radiance of the glory' (Heb. 1:3). This is the greatness and excellence of beauty in its perfection. In this sense, the infinite excellence of God, in his inconceivable perfections, raised in such brightness as to exceed completely all our apprehensions, is called his 'glory.' He is therefore 'The God of glory' (Acts 7:2), the most glorious God; our Saviour is called 'the Lord of glory' (1 Cor. 2:8), in the same sense. In this respect we can give no glory to God; we can add nothing to his excellencies, nor to the infinite, inconceivable brightness of them, by anything that we do.

(b) Glory relates not only to the thing itself, but to the estimation and view we have of it; that is, when something which is in itself glorious is also esteemed to be so. The Roman philosopher Cicero says, '*Glory is frequented by someone with praise,*' or '*The united expression of approval by the good, the genuine testimony of men who have the power of forming a proper judgment of virtuous conduct.*' In this respect something which is infinitely glorious in itself may become more or less glorious as it is revealed, and by the estimation made of it. With this sense, glory is not one of God's excellencies or perfections, but is the esteem and manifestation of them among, and towards, others.

God himself declares that this is his glory. Moses wished to see God's 'glory.' God called this 'his face'; that is, the glory of God in itself. 'This,' said God, 'you cannot see. "You cannot see my face," the brightness of my essential glory, the splendour of my excellencies and perfections.' What then? Is Moses not to have any knowledge at all of God's glory? God placed him in a rock and told him that there he would show him his glory. And this he did, referring to that glory as 'my back'; that is, he declared to him where and how his glory is manifested (Exod. 33:18-23). Now, this Rock that followed them was Christ (1 Cor. 10:4). The Lord placed Moses in that rock to show him his glory; implying that there is no glimpse of God's glory to be obtained except by those who are placed in Christ Jesus. What is this glory of God which he showed to Moses? We are told in Exodus 34:6-8, that he, causing his majesty, or some visible signs of his presence, to 'pass before him,' proclaimed the name of God, with many gracious properties of his nature and blessedness. It is as if he had said, 'Moses, do you want to see my glory? This is it: that I may be known to be "The Lord, the Lord, a God merciful and gracious." Let me be known to be this, and that is the glory that I require from the sons of men.'

You see, therefore, how steadfastness in believing gives glory to God. It sets forth and magnifies all these properties of God and gives all his attributes their due praise.

It manifests a high estimation of them. Let me enter into detail here. I could show that there is not one property of God, by which he has made himself known to us, that is not given the glory due to it, to some degree, by steadfast believing. It would be easy to show how this gives God the glory of his faithfulness, truth, power, righteousness, grace, mercy, goodness, love, patience, and whatever else God has revealed himself to be. Conversely, all doubts arise when we call some divine attribute into question.

Here is the force of this first testimony: if the glory of God is all that he requires at our hands, and steadfastness in believing, and this alone, gives him this glory, it must necessarily be pleasing to him.

(ii) A testimony of similar significance is found in Hebrews 6:17, 18. 'The heirs of the promise,' those to whom the great promise of Christ is made, are believers. They are said here to have 'fled for refuge,' the 'fliers with speed.' The expression is clearly metaphorical. Some say that the reference is to those who run in a race for a prize. This is suggested, they say, by the Greek word used which means 'to take a fast hold of.' Runners in a race, when they reach the line, seize the prize and hold on to it tightly.

Our translators, by rendering the word 'fleeing for refuge,' show that they understand it in terms of men guilty of manslaughter in the Old Testament flying to the city of refuge. Many other translators choose the same rendering. I believe this is the correct choice for two reasons:

(a) Because I think the apostle, when writing to Hebrews about an institution of God, would more readily refer to a

[23]

Hebrew custom, particularly one so relevant to the topic under discussion, than to a custom of the Greeks and Romans in their races, which had so much less relevance.

(b) Because the context of the phrase so clearly suggests a fleeing from something as well as a flying to something. In this respect, the verse tells us that there is an encouragement for them; namely, their deliverance from the evil which they feared and fled from. In a race, a prize is certainly offered, but there is no evil avoided. It was different for him who fled for refuge: he had a city of safety before him but also an avenger of blood behind him. He fled with speed and diligence to the one in order to avoid the other. These cities of refuge were provided for the manslayer who, having killed a man by accident and therefore finding himself in sudden danger – for it was lawful for an avenger of blood to slay him – might flee with all his strength to one of those cities where he might enjoy immunity and safety.

In this way, a poor sinner, finding himself in a condition of guilt and surprised by the sense of it, seeing death and destruction ready to seize him, flies with all his strength to the embrace of the Lord Jesus, the only city of refuge from the avenging justice of God and curse of the law. This *flying* to the embrace of Christ – the hope set before us for relief and safety – is believing. It is called here *flying* by the Holy Spirit to express its nature to the spiritual sense of believers. What happens now? Does Christ respond to this 'flying for refuge,' that is, their believing? Indeed, he takes every means possible to demonstrate how abundantly willing he is to receive them. He has engaged his word and his promise, that they might not doubt or stagger in the least but know that he is ready to receive them and to give them 'strong encouragement.' And what is this encouragement? How will it arise? How was he who had slain a man by accident and had fled to the city of refuge encouraged? Wasn't it by this: that the gates of the city would certainly be open for him, that he would find protection there and be safe from the avenger? From where, then, must our strong encouragement come if we fly for refuge by believing? It will surely come from God who is ready to receive us; that he will in no way shut us out but will welcome us, and that the greater our speed in coming, the more welcome we shall be. He assures us of this by engaging his word and oath to that end. What further testimony could we have that our believing is acceptable to him?

It is said, 'If [any man] shrinks back, [the Lord] has no pleasure in him' (Heb. 10:38). What is it to shrink back? It is to fall away from steadfastness in believing. This is how the apostle interprets it: 'We are not of those who shrink back, but of those who have faith' (verse 39). Drawing back is the opposite of having faith. In these who shrink back and do not maintain their steadfastness in believing, nor make every effort to do so, the Lord's 'soul has no pleasure'; that is, he greatly abhors and abominates them (which is the meaning of that expression). His delight is in those who are steadfast in adhering to the promises; in them his soul takes pleasure.

When the Jews discussed salvation with our Saviour, they asked him, 'What must we do, to be doing the works of God?' (John 6:28); that work of God by which they might be accepted by him. This is the cry of every convicted person. Our Saviour's answer was, 'This is the work of God, that you believe in him who he has sent' (verse 29). 'Do you wish to know the great work by which God is delighted?' he asks them. 'This is it: that you believe and be firm in your belief.'

Hence the many exhortations that are given to us by the Holy Spirit on this matter: verses such as Hebrews 12:12; Isa. 35. But I need not provide further testimonies out of the many examples provided for us.

2. *The next confirmation of my proposition consists in further applications of the testimony of Scripture that God is glorified by our steadfastness in believing.*

It is granted by all that God's ultimate purpose in everything he does himself, and all that he requires us to do, is his own glory. It cannot be otherwise if he is the first, the only independent being, the prime cause of all things and their chief good. Having placed his glory in that which cannot be achieved and brought about without believing, according to the present constitution of things, God, therefore, must find belief acceptable; just as any wise and righteous person will find a suitable means to achieve a designed purpose to be acceptable.

Bear in mind, please, what I mean by believing. Though the word may be used widely and generally, in this discussion I am limiting it to the specific meaning of that continuing establishing of our souls in the receiving of Jesus Christ, offered to us in the truth and from the love of the Father, for the pardon of sins and the acceptance of our persons before God. It is this that is necessary, according to God's constitution of things in the covenant of grace, to bring about that design of glory to himself, which he intends. He therefore sums up his whole purpose as being 'the praise of his glorious grace' (Eph. 1:6).

In Proverbs 25:2, if I am not mistaken, this is clearly expressed: 'It is the glory of God to conceal things,' or 'to cover a matter.' I have already told you what constitutes the glory of God. It is not the splendour and majesty of his infinite and excellent perfections, arising not from anything he does, but from what he is; but it is the exaltation and demonstration of the essence of those excellencies. When God is received, is believed, is known to be such as he declares himself, then is he glorified – that is his glory. And in this verse, says the Holy Spirit, this glory arises by him 'concealing things,' by 'covering a matter.'

What is being spoken about here? It is not that it is the glory of God to conceal everything. On the contrary, it is his glory to 'bring to light the things now hidden in darkness' (1 Cor. 4:5). The manifestation of his own works declares his glory (Psa. 19:1). So does the manifestation of the good works of his people (Matt. 5:16). It must be things of some specific nature that are referred to here. We are helped to understand what these are by the second half of the proverb: 'The glory of kings is to search things out' (Prov. 25:2). What kind of things is it the glory of kings to discover? Isn't it faults and offences against the law? It is to the glory of magistrates to search out transgressions, so that those transgressions may be punished. Their glory is to inquire, find out, and punish offences, transgressions of the law. It is, therefore, sinful things – sin itself – which it is the glory of God to conceal. But what does 'concealing a sinful thing' mean? It is the opposite of the searching out of the magistrate, of which we have a full description in Job 29:16, 17 (KJV): 'The cause which I knew not I searched out. And I brake the jaws of the wicked.' It is to conduct judicial inquiries, to search out hidden transgressions, so that the offenders might be brought to a deserved punishment. God's concealing a thing is therefore his work of not searching out sins and sinners with the purpose of punishing them, to make them naked to the stroke of the law. It is his hiding of sin from the condemning power of the law.

The word used here is the same as that which David uses, 'Blessed is the one ... whose sin is covered' (Psa. 32:1). In many other scriptures it is used in the same way. In Micah 7:19, for example: God will 'cast all our sins into the depths of the sea.' Anything so disposed of is utterly covered from the sight of men. God, by these words, expresses the truth that the sins of his people will be out of sight and will not bring them to judgment; they will be 'cast into the depths of the sea.' Similarly, in the New Testament, our sins are said to be 'forgiven.' The basic meaning of the original word in the Greek is 'to remove' or 'dismiss' something; 'to send, or remove, our sins out of sight.' It is the same in substance as the word used in Proverbs 25 and translated 'conceal.' It is used in another context in Matthew 23:23: 'You have *neglected* the weightier matters of the law'; that is, you have laid them aside, out of sight, as it were, taking no care of them.

At the heart of all these expressions of *removing*, *hiding*, *covering* and *concealing* sin, giving light and significance to them, relating them to forgiveness of sin, is the reference they make to the mercy seat under the law. The construction and use of this seat are described in Exodus 35:17, 18. It was a plate of pure gold, lying on the ark, and called in Hebrew 'a covering.' In the ark was the law, written on tables of stone. Over the mercy seat, between the cherubim, was the oracle representing God. By this, the Holy Spirit signified that the mercy seat was to cover the law, together with its condemning power, as it were, from the eye of God's justice, so that we might not be consumed. In this way, God is said to cover sin, in that, by the mercy seat he hides the strength and power of sin, as far as its guilt and liability to punishment is concerned. The apostle calls this mercy seat '*to hilastērion*' (Heb. 9:5). The word appears again only once in the New Testament, where it is used as a reference to Christ: 'Whom God put forward as a *propitiation* ('as a mercy seat')' (Rom. 3:25). Only Christ is that mercy seat by whom sin and the law, which gives sin its strength, is hidden. It is from this typological use that we have the expression in the Old Testament, 'Hide me in the shadow of your wings' (Psa. 17:8), referring to the wings of the cherubim where the mercy seat was; that is, hide me in the embrace of Christ.

Now, says the Holy Spirit, to hide, to cover, to pardon sin by Christ, in this way, is the glory of God, in which he will be exalted and admired, and for which he will be praised. Give him this, and you give him his great purpose and design. Let him be believed in and trusted as God in Christ pardoning iniquity, transgression and sin – so reconciling the world to himself and manifesting his glorious properties – and he achieves his purpose.

If I were now to proceed by showing what God has done, what he does, and what he will do, in setting up his glory, it would demonstrate clearly that this is what he aims at. His eternal electing love lies at the bottom of this purpose. This is what it tends to: that God might be glorified in the forgiveness of sin. The sending of his Son – an inscrutable mystery of wisdom, goodness and righteousness – together with all that the Son did and suffered, by God's authority and commission, was all for the purpose of the glorifying of God in it. Has the new covenant of grace any other purpose? Didn't God deliberately propose, draw up and establish that covenant in the blood of his Son? By his works of creation and providence he had, through the old covenant and law, given glory to himself in other respects; now, by this, he glorifies himself by the forgiving of iniquity. The dispensation of the Holy Spirit for the conversion of sinners, with all the mighty works resulting from it, is designed for the same purpose. Why does God exercise such patience, forbearance, longsuffering towards us, for which he will be admired to all eternity and at the thought of which our souls stand amazed? It is all in order that he may bring about this glory of his: the covering of iniquity and the pardoning of sin.

What is it, then, that is required on our part that this great design for his glory may be accomplished in us and towards us? Isn't it our believing and our steadfastness in belief? I do not need to stay to prove this, or to give further light and strength to my conclusion from what has been said; namely, that if these things are true, then our believing and steadfastness in belief are exceedingly acceptable to God.

3. *For the third and last demonstration of this point, I shall mention one further detail of God's pursuit of his glory, and that is his institution and command of preaching the gospel to all nations, and the great care he has taken to provide those*

who will be the instruments for the propagation of this gospel and who will proclaim the word of his grace by it. 'Go therefore and make disciples of all nations' (Matt. 28:19); 'Proclaim the gospel to the whole creation' (Mark 16:15).

What is this gospel which he commands to be preached and declared? It is the declaration of his mind and will of his gracious acceptance of all believing and of all steadfastness in believing. God declares his purpose, his eternal unchangeable will, that there is, by his appointment, an infallible and inviolable connection between believing in Jesus Christ and receiving him together with everlasting fruit in him. He declares this to all. His purpose to bestow faith relates effectually only to some: they 'believed who were appointed to eternal life' (Acts 13:48). But this purpose of his will – that believing in Jesus Christ will bring about righteousness and salvation in the enjoyment of himself – concerns all alike. For what purpose, then, has the Lord taken care that this gospel should be preached and declared in this way until the end of the world, other than that our believing is acceptable to him?

But I will stop from presenting more demonstrations, in which so many things offer themselves to our consideration, so that I might not be detained any longer from my main purpose in these two sermons.

Sermon 2

The Strength of Faith (*cont.*)

*No distrust made him waver concerning the promise of God,
but he grew strong in his faith as he gave glory to God.*
—Rom. 4:20

THE application of this sermon is to encourage the duty
commanded and exalted in the text; that is, I shall present
motives for steadfastness in believing the promises. Out of
the many that are usually brought forward for this purpose
I shall mention those that seem to me to be the most
effective.

Application 1

We shall begin by considering God himself, in the person
of the Father, and his declaration, made of himself in Christ
Jesus, of his love, kindness, tenderness, readiness and willingness to receive poor sinners. The rest and peace of our
souls in holding on to him by believing will depend on our
apprehensions both of him and of the thoughts of his heart
towards us. In human company we are free and easy with
those whom we know to be of a kind, loving, compassion-
ate disposition, but full of doubts, fears and jealousies when

we have to deal with those who are morose, irritable and difficult. Entertaining hard thoughts of God always ends in continually seeking to escape, and maintaining a distance, from him and to give ourselves to anything in the world rather than to be dealing and conversing with him. What delight can anyone take in someone whom he conceives to be always angry, wrathful, ready to destroy? What comforting expectation can anyone have from such a person? Consider therefore, in some detail, how God describes himself, and as you think of these things, judge whether or not it might be profitable to encourage your hearts to be steadfast in believing the promises, and in embracing the Son of his love offered in them:

(i) He gives us his name as a support for us (Isa. 50:10). He speaks to poor, dejected, bewildered, fainting sinners: 'Do not give up; do not let go your hold. Though you might be in darkness with regard to all other means of support and comfort, yet "trust in the name of the Lord." And should you do so, this name will be "a strong tower" to you' (Prov. 18:10). The nature of this name of God which is such a support and safe defence is described fully in Exod. 34:6, 7. It is that name which he promised to show to Moses. To be known by this name is that glory of God in which he aims to be exalted. Indeed, God is so fully known by his name, and the whole of the obedience that he requires from us is so ordered and directed in its revelation, that when our Saviour had declared him and all his will to us, he summed up his work by the following words: 'I have manifested your name to the people whom you gave me out of the world' (John 17:6). The manifestation of the name of God to the elect was the great work of Christ on the earth, as prophet and teacher of his church. He declared the name of God – his gracious, loving, tender nature – his blessed attributes, suited to encourage poor creatures to come to him and to trust in him. This, then, is the name of him in whom we are to believe – the name which he has given to us by which to call him – that we might deal with him as the one described by his name. He is gracious, loving, ready to pity, help, receive us. He delights in our good and rejoices in our approach to him. This is what he has proclaimed of himself; this is what his only Son has revealed him to be. He is not called Apollyon, a destroyer, but the Saviour of men. Why would anyone not trust in him, by the way which he himself has appointed and approved?

(ii) As is his name, so is his nature. He says of himself 'I have no wrath' (Isa. 27:4). He is speaking with reference to his church, to believers. With regard to you, there is no such thing as that anger or wrath in God, of which you are in such fear. Have you had hard thoughts of him? Have you been harbouring frightening reports of him, as though he were a devouring fire and endless burnings? 'Do not be mistaken,' he says. 'I have no wrath.' He does not have one wrathful, revengeful thought towards you. No; take hold of his protection and you shall have peace' (verse 5). He is love – he is of an infinitely loving and tender nature – all love. There is nothing in him that is inconsistent with love itself. We know how a little love, a weak affection in man's nature, will affect a tender father in his relationship towards his child. How it melted, softened and reconciled the father of the prodigal in the parable! 'O my son Absalom! Would that I had died instead of you,' said David, a poor father in distress at the death of a rebellious child. A child will bear himself up above fear and terror, even after many mistakes, knowing of the love of a tender father. What then shall we say, or think, of Him who is love in the abstract – whose nature is love? May we not conclude that he is 'merciful and gracious, slow to anger and abounding in steadfast love' (Psa. 103:8)? As we are led, by degrees, into an acquaintance with God in his attributes (for we are led into it by steps and stages, not being able, all at once, to bear all the glory which he is pleased to shine here upon us), so are we amazed by his different glories. An experience of any one of the attributes of God as discovered in Christ, and acting for our good, greatly encourages the soul, but none more than this: that he is love and ready to forgive us on that account. This is the church's condition: 'Who is a God like you, pardoning iniquity and passing over transgression?' (Mic. 7:18). Can it enter a man's heart? O who is like him? Is it possible that he should deal with sinners in this way? This discovery overwhelms the soul and strengthens it in faith and trust in him.

There is a general compassion in God by which his providential ways are governed, which is too difficult for men to apprehend when they come across it. Poor Jonah was angry that he was so merciful (Jonah 4:2): 'I knew that you were not one that I could deal with. You are so gracious and merciful, slow to anger and abounding with steadfast love, and relenting from disaster, that it is not for me, with any credit or reputation, to be engaged and employed in your work and service.' And if God is so full of compassion to the world, which today is alive, and tomorrow is to be

thrown into the fire, is he not much more tender to you,
O you of little faith? When dealing with God, therefore, fit
the thoughts of your hearts to this revelation which he has
made of his own nature. He is good – love and kindness
itself; there is no wrath in him – he is ready to forgive,
accept and embrace.

(iii) His dealings with us and actions towards us are according to his name and his nature. For one who has such a
name, and is disposed in such a way towards us, we should
expect that his actions will be carried out with great readiness and cheerfulness, expressing that name and nature.
'How then will he demonstrate this and make it evident?'
He will have mercy. He is love; he will have mercy. Truly,
'he will abundantly pardon' (Isa. 55:7). 'But how will he do
it?' Ah, you cannot imagine how! His thoughts are not your
thoughts (verse 8). You have poor, low, mean thoughts of
God's way of pardoning. You cannot reach or comprehend
it in any way. However great your ability to understand, you
will never come near to it. 'As the heavens are higher than
the earth, so are my ways higher than your ways and my
thoughts than your thoughts' (verse 9). 'But does God, then,
not pardon as we do? Begrudgingly, after many persuasions,
and eventually doing so "with an unwilling kind of willingness," so that honest souls can hardly distinguish between
our wrath and our pardon?' Not at all. What he does, he
does with his whole heart and his whole soul (Jer. 32:41);
and he rejoices in doing so (Zeph. 3:17). He will have mercy,
he will abundantly pardon; he will do it with his whole soul;
he will rejoice in doing so and quieten you in his love. I do
not know what more we could ask for, as an assurance of

his free acceptance of us. You will say, perhaps, that this only happens on occasions and that we are fortunate if we approach him at such times. No, for such actions of his are in accordance with his name and his nature. His whole heart and his whole soul are in it. He will therefore plan out his steps to accomplish it. 'He will wait to be gracious to you' (Isa. 30:18). His heart is set upon it and he will take every opportunity to fulfil his desire and design. And if our stubbornness and folly are such as to almost wear out his patience – to make him weary, as he complains (Isa. 43:24), and to cause him to stretch beyond the limits of his patience – he will exalt himself, take to himself his great power so as to remove our stubbornness, so that he might be merciful to us. One way or another, he will fulfil the desire of his heart, the purpose of his grace.

To explain this truth further, consider these further aspects of God's dealing with us, and of his graciousness towards us, as he acts according to his own name and nature:

(a) He compares himself to creatures possessing the most tender and boundless affection: 'Can a woman forget her nursing child?' (Isa. 49:15, 16). This is as high as we can go. The affection of a mother to a nursing child, the child of her womb, is the utmost example that we can give of love, tenderness and affection. 'You cannot think,' says God, 'you ought not to imagine, that a tender, loving mother should not have compassion on "the son of her womb." Things will act according to their natures – even tigers love their offspring – and shall a woman forget her nursing child?' 'But yet,' says God, 'if you can raise your imagination to this, take it for granted that she may do so (which, however, cannot be imagined without offering violence to nature), "yet I will not forget you" – this will not reach my love, my affection.' Were we as certain of the love of God to us as we are of the love of a good, gracious mother to her nursing child, whom we see embracing it and rejoicing over it all day long, we would think our situation very secure and comfortable. But, alas, what is this love compared to God's love to the meanest saint on earth! What is a drop to an ocean? What is a little dying, decaying affection to an infinity, an eternity of love? Notice how this love of God acts, as described in Hosea 11:8, 9 and Jeremiah 31:20.

(b) He stoops down to plead with us that it may be so, that he may exercise pity, pardon, goodness, kindness, mercy towards us. He is so full that he is, as it were, in pain until he can get us to himself so as to communicate his love to us. 'We implore you,' says the apostle, 'on behalf of Christ … God making his appeal through us' (2 Cor. 5:20). What is he appealing for? What is he so concerned about? Clearly some great thing, some difficult task. 'No,' he says, 'but "be reconciled to God."' God says, 'O sons of men, why will you die? I beseech you, be friends with me. Let us agree. Accept the atonement. I have love for you; take mercy, take pardon. Do not destroy your own souls.' 'This is rest; give rest to the weary; and this is repose' (Isa. 28:12). Recall how the Scriptures abound with exhortations and pleas, all aiming at the same object.

(c) In condescending to our weakness, he has added his oath to this end. Will you not believe him? Will you not trust him? Are we afraid that if we give ourselves up to him, place ourselves in his hands, he will kill us? That we will die? He gives to us the ultimate guarantee against such fearful thoughts. The most that anyone can ask when, full of fears, he gives himself up to someone who is stronger than him, is: 'Swear to me that I shall not die.' 'As I live, declares the Lord God, I have no pleasure in the death of the wicked' (Ezek. 33:11). I think that this should put an end to all argument. We have his promise and oath (Heb. 6:17, 18); what more do we want? He is of an infinitely loving and tender nature; he pleads with us to come to him; he swears that we shall not suffer by doing so. Innumerable similar examples might be given as evidence that God acts towards us according to his name and nature.

My aim in all these considerations is to encourage our hearts to believe the promises. We are dealing with God when we accept the promises. The things we receive on believing are excellent, desirable, all that we want, things which will do us good to all eternity. The difficulties of believing spring from our own unworthiness and from our terror of him with whom we are dealing. To disentangle our souls from the power of such thoughts and fears, this is what is emphasised: the tender, gracious, loving nature of him with whom we have to do. Fill your hearts with these kind of thoughts about God; exercise your minds with this understanding of him. The psalmist tells us the result of doing so: 'Those who know your name put their trust in you' (Psa. 9:10); a strengthening of faith will follow. If we know the name of God, as he has revealed it – know the love and kindness wrapped up in it – we cannot help trusting him. If we always think of God with a clear persuasion that he is gracious, loving, ready to receive us, delighting, rejoicing to embrace us, to do us good, to give us mercy and glory – to give whatever he has promised in Jesus Christ – it will greatly help to establish our hearts.

But great caution must be exercised with respect to all that has been said. I have not been speaking of the general aspect of God's nature, but of the goodness and love of God towards his people in Jesus Christ. Therefore, to clear the matter further and to establish a firm foundation for this truth, I wish to add the following observations:

1. I acknowledge that everything that can be said by all the sons of men concerning the goodness, loveliness and kindness of God in his own blessed nature, is inconceivably, infinitely, below what it is in reality. How small a fraction is all that we know of his goodness! Though we have all his works and all his word to teach us, yet, just as we have no affections large enough to embrace it, so we have no faculty able to receive or apprehend it. Admiration – that state when the soul is nonplussed,[1] hardly knows what it is doing and so comes to a standstill, ready to break – is all that we can arrive at when we contemplate it. His excellencies and perfections of goodness and love are sufficient to engage the love and obedience of all rational creatures, and when they can go no further they may, with the psalmist, call upon all their fellow-creatures to help them in the work. Nor can any man exercise himself in a more noble contemplation than that of the beauty and loveliness of God. 'How great is his goodness! How great is his beauty!' Those who have nothing but awful, harsh apprehensions of the nature of God – that he is unjustifiably severe and wrathful – do

---

[1] Owen uses the phrase *the soul's 'non-plus'* (Latin for 'no more').

not know him. It is unjustifiable, unreasonable and wicked to think of him as cruel and bloodthirsty, to make use of his greatness only in order to frighten, terrify and destroy the works of his hands, for he is good and does good. He made all things good, in beauty and order, and loves all the things he has made. He has filled everything that we see and apprehend with the fruits of his goodness. If you consider God and all his works as he made them and in the order that he assigned to them, you will find nothing in his nature towards you except kindness, gentleness, goodness, power (exerted to maintain the flow of his goodness towards you), grace and bounty, in daily, continued supplies.

But, alas, we are talking of sinners. It is true that in God, as he is by nature, there is an abundant excellence and beauty, a ravishing goodness and love for his creatures to love. As he made them, they could desire nothing more; the sin of some of them was their failure to love him above everything for his loveliness, for the suitableness of his excellencies to bind their hearts to him as their chief and only good.[2] But upon the entrance of sin the whole state of things is changed. God, truly, is not changed; his glories and perfections are the same from eternity to eternity, but the creature is changed, and what was desirable and loveable to him before, ceases to be so, though it remained so in itself. He who had boldness before God – who was neither afraid nor ashamed – while he stood in the law of his creation, after he had sinned, trembled at the hearing of God's voice. He even tried to separate from him for ever and to hide from him. What attribute of God was more lovely to his creatures than his holiness? How glorious, lovely, desirable above all is

[2] A reference, perhaps, to the fallen angels.

he to those who remain in his image and likeness! But as for sinners, they cannot serve him because of his holiness (Josh. 24:19). In the revelation of God to sinners, together with the discovery of his goodness, kindness and graciousness, there is also a vision given of his justice, wrath, anger, severity and indignation against sin. These form an unconquerable barrier between the sinner and all the fruits that flow from goodness and love. Hence, instead of being drawn to God, their response is that of Micah 6:6, 7: 'With what shall I come before the Lord, and bow myself before God on high? Shall I come before him with burnt offerings, with calves a year old?', and when convicted of the impossibility of the success of any such attempt, they cry out 'Who among us can dwell with the consuming fire' (Isa. 33:14). A desire to avoid him to all eternity is all that a sinner's best consideration of God, in his essential excellencies, can lead him to. For who would send thorns to battle with him? Who would bring the driest stubble to a consuming fire? This is why those who believe in general grace as a ground of hope for sinners, on the basis of the natural goodness of God, when they come to answer the objection, 'But God is just, as well as merciful,' with many good words, take away with one hand just as much as they give with the other. 'Consider,' they say, 'God's gracious nature; he is good to all. Trust this. Do not believe those who say otherwise.' But he is just also and will not let sin go unpunished. He must therefore punish sin according to its demerit. Where, now, therefore, is the hope spoken of? Because of this, notice:

2. That since the entrance of sin there is no apprehension by sinners of a goodness, love and kindness in God flowing

from his natural attributes, except when due to the inter-position of his sovereign will and pleasure. What some say – that special grace flows from what they call general grace and special mercy from general mercy – is completely false. There is a whole nest of mistakes in that conception. God's sovereign distinguishing will is the fountain of all special grace and mercy. 'I will,' he says, 'make all my goodness pass before you,' and 'I will have mercy on whom I have mercy' (Exod. 33:19; Rom. 9:15). Here is the fountain of mercy: the will of God. He is of a merciful and gracious nature but dispenses mercy and grace by his sovereign will. It is electing love that is at the bottom of all special grace, all special kindness; by this the elect are established when the rest are hardened (Rom. 11:7). He blesses us with spiritual blessings even as he has chosen us (Eph. 1:3, 4). God, having made all things good, and imparted of the fruits of his goodness to all those who sinned and came short of his glory, might, without the least injury to, or restraint of, his own goodness, have given them over to an everlasting separation from him. That he deals otherwise with any of them is not from any tendency in his nature and goodness to relieve them, but from his sovereign, wise, gracious will, in which he freely purposed in himself to do them good by Jesus Christ (Eph. 1:9).

I say then that all considerations of the goodness and mercifulness of the nature of God, and of general grace arising from it, are so balanced in the soul of a sinner by considerations of his justice and severity – so weakened by the experience that all men have that these are not extended effectively for the good of all who are imagined to have a right to them – that, when viewed in this way, they provide no basis for comfort to sinners. And if anyone would attempt to approach God on the basis of this general grace, he would meet with the sword of justice long before drawing near to him. So that:

3. Where the Scriptures mention the goodness of God by which he reveals himself to be love, to be gracious and tender, it is not on account of his perfections considered in himself, but on the new and special basis of the free engagement of his attributes in Christ with regard to the elect. These scriptural references, to the extent that they speak of spiritual matters and are not restricted to the ways of providence, belong to the covenant of grace and to God manifested in Christ. This is what is meant by those writers who say that it is not from the natural goodness of God that he is good to sinners, but from his gracious will. If it were not for that, all communications of good to sinners would be ended forever.

This, then, is what we must seek: the gracious nature of God, the Father, as revealed in Christ on the basis of the atonement made for sin. This is the One whom the poor weak believer has to do with. This is he who invites us to accept Christ in his promises. Here is the Principal with whom we have to deal in everything concerned with our redemption. He is love; ready, willing to receive and embrace all those who come to him by Christ. If we become convinced of his goodwill, kindness and patience towards us, we will certainly be established in our belief in the faithfulness of his promises.

4. Notice again who it is of whom I am speaking. It is believers, those who have a belief in God by Christ. Let others, then (those who do not believe), be careful not to

abuse and wrest the doctrine of the grace of God to their own destruction. I know that nothing is more common with men of vain, light spirits, formalists and even presumptuous sinners, than to say and think, 'God is merciful; there is still good hope on that basis. He did not make men in order to damn them, and whatever preachers say, it will, or at least, it *may* be well with us at the end.' But, poor creatures, even this God of whom we have been speaking 'is a consuming fire; a God of purer eyes than to see evil.' A God who will not let the least sin go unpunished. And the greater his love, his goodness, his condescension to those who come to him on his own terms by Christ, the greater will be his wrath and indignation against those who refuse his offer of love in his own way, and yet say 'I shall be safe, though I walk in the stubbornness of my heart' (Deut. 29:19).

Application 2

A second motive for being steadfast in our faith in the promises may be taken from the glories of the Lord Jesus Christ to whom, by believing, we draw near and receive. Now, the wonders of his person are such, they not only encourage us to come to him to possess them, but they are all suited to help us as we come: to support us and make us steadfast in our belief.[3]

Application 3

In the same way, we may consider the promises of God, in which both his love and the excellence and suitableness of

---

[3] On this point, with its many aspects, see Owen's book, *Of Communion with God the Father, Son, and Holy Ghost*, Part II, Chapter III, Digression I, *Works*, vol. 2 (Edinburgh: Banner of Truth Trust, 1976), pp. 59-79.

the Lord Jesus Christ are clearly and eminently expressed. Many things are spoken of the promises to very good effect: their nature, stability, preciousness, efficacy, all centred in one covenant, all confirmed in Christ. These are all matters with which the soul particularly engages when believing. I shall presently mention two things:

(i) The infinite graciousness of the Lord seen in *his use of the promises to forestall all the objections and fears* of our unbelieving hearts.

(ii) The manifestation of his wisdom and love in *fitting the promises to the most urgent needs, troubles, anxieties and fears* of our souls, so that we clearly see his intention to help us by them.

(i) We could demonstrate the first of these from various kinds of examples. I will mention one only and that is the *unexpected relief* that is found in them for us: the way they offer grace and mercy when these would seem to be the last thing in the world to be looked for. We may see this, and the use made of it, by considering some particular well-known promises.

(a) *Isaiah 43:22–26*: We have here persons who are guilty of various sinful follies. The Lord accuses them sharply, convicting their consciences. He does not spare them from wounds and blows. They had neglected his worship and not called on his name. Though they could not put aside all performance of duties, yet what they did was burdensome to them. They were tired of worship – tired of God in it – and of all spiritual communion and converse with him. 'You have been weary of me' (verse 22). Their convictions compelled them to do God some service, but it was, as we say, death to them. They were weary of it. They utterly neglected most of the things that God required, both the matter and the manner of them. What, then, will God say of himself with reference to their behaviour? 'Notwithstanding all my patience, you have made me weary of you. I am like someone who has had hard service, and who cannot abide it. It is a bondage,' says God, 'for me to have anything to do with you.' Suppose we now were those poor souls, fully convinced that this is our state before God; our unbelief and corruption so strong that we are weary of God and his ways. It may be that we have faint desires that things might be otherwise and therefore we bind ourselves to perform our duties in the hope that God might be flattered. However, because of our innumerable follies, God also is weary of us, so that we can no longer bear our bondage to him any longer. We are weary of serving. What can such poor sinners conclude except that everlasting separation from God must be the ultimate end? They are weary of God, and God is weary of them. Surely, then, they must part, and part forever. What remedy is there, or can be? Poor soul! Lie down in darkness.

But look how God actually responds! What unexpected grace is found in his word of promise. Is it, 'Be gone. Take a bill of divorce. Follow your own course, and I will follow mine against you'? 'No,' says God. 'Here is a situation of which I am weary and you are weary. I am weary of your multiplying the guilt of sin. You are wearied in serving the power of sin. I will put an end to this situation. We will have peace again between us. I will blot out your transgressions and will not remember your sins. I, even I, will do it.' He repeats the word passionately, emphatically, so as to remind us with whom we are dealing in this situation. 'I, I am he. Who am God and not man. I – who am great in mercy and who will abundantly pardon – I will do it.'

'But,' says the poor convicted soul, 'I do not know of any reason why you should do so. I cannot believe it, because I do not know of any reason why I should be dealt with in this way.' 'I know very well that there is nothing in you which explains why I should deal with you in this way,' says God. 'What you deserve is to be eternally cut off. But quieten your heart. I will do it for my own sake. I have deeper engagements on my own account in this matter than you are able to apprehend.'

No doubt, such a word as this, being issued when God and the soul were at the point of ending all fellowship – when the soul was certainly ready to do so, and had great cause to think that God would be the first to break connection – being pronounced, against all expectation and above all hopes, would cause the soul to cry out, like Thomas at the sight of Christ's wounds: 'My Lord and my God.' Let the soul that fails to maintain any steadfastness in believing in Christ and in the promises, that staggers and is tossed to and fro between hopes and fears, being filled with a sense of sin and unworthiness, dwell a while on the thought of this unexpected response and give itself up to its power.

(b) *Isaiah 57:17, 18*: These verses provide another similar example. There seems to be here a description of a man who has been totally rejected by God. The most dejected sinner can hardly present a more deplorable description of his condition, though ready enough to speak of all the evil of his heart that he is aware of. Let us take note of his state. There is an iniquity found in him and upon him which God abhors. This evil is of such long standing that God is provoked to address it. 'I was angry,' says God, 'and took steps to let him know it. I laid my hand upon him and struck him by some unwelcome providence so that he could not avoid realising that I was angry. He responded when struck; perhaps he began to look for me and to pray; but he did not find me, for I hid myself. I let him pray but took no notice of him and hid myself from him in my wrath. Surely he will now leave his iniquity and return to me. No,' says God, 'he grows worse than ever: neglecting my blows, hiding, angry, he continues perversely in the way of his own heart.'

God had appointed in the law that when a son was rebellious against his parents and had become fixed in this behaviour, he should be 'stoned with stones.' What should be done, then, with this person who is similarly incorrigible under God's hand? God answers, '"I have seen his ways" (verse 18), he will not improve. Shall I destroy him, consume him, and make him as Admah and Zeboiim? Ah, "my heart recoils within me; my compassion grows warm and tender" (Hos. 11:8). "I will heal him." If he continues in this way and no help be given him to do him good, he will perish; but "I will heal him." He wounded his soul; I also wounded him by the blows I gave him when I was angry. Is he not "my dear son? ... For as often as I speak against him, I do remember him still. Therefore, my heart yearns for him; I will surely have mercy on him"' (Jer. 31:20). He shall have wine and oil, grace and pardon, for all his wounds. But, alas, he is unable to take one step in God's ways, he is so addicted to his own. 'Leave that to me,' says God; 'I will lead him, and restore comfort to him.'

If there is anyone who cannot, to some degree, apply this promise to his own condition, then things are very hard with him indeed. I know the necessity of that duty and usefulness of searching our hearts for the fruits of the Spirit in us, by which we are made fit for communion with God, and which are evidences of our acceptance with him and of the pardon of our sins. Yet, it is still true that these are promises that provide a sufficient warrant for a perplexed soul to draw near to Christ, offered as they are by the love of the Father, even when that soul can find no other qualifications or conditions, other than those which make him unworthy in every way to be accepted. We do not say to a poor, naked, hungry, homeless man, 'Go, find clothes for yourself, find food, find a home, and then I will give you alms.' No, but rather, 'Because you do not have these things, I will, therefore, give you alms.' 'Because you are poor, blind, polluted, guilty, sinful,' says God, 'I will give you mercy.'

It is true that before a man believes in the promise it is necessary for him to feel and acknowledge his state and condition. This must be the case when receiving the promise (often it is, itself, the fruit and work of the gift of the promise). But as to the offer of the promise, and to the offer of Christ in the promise, this is not so. When did God give that great promise of Christ to Adam? Was it when he was sorrowing, repenting, admitting the state of his soul? No, but when he was flying, hiding, and had no thoughts of anything except separation from God. God calls him out, tells him immediately what he deserves, pronounces the curse, and gives him the blessing. 'Under the apple tree I awakened you. There your mother was in labour with you' (Song of Sol. 8:5). From the very place of sin, there Christ raises up the soul. We find this again in Isa. 46:12: 'Listen to me, you stubborn of heart, you who are far from righteousness.' What would we say of these two notable qualifications? Stubbornness and being far from righteousness. But what does God say to them? He speaks to them of mercy and salvation (verse 13). Or again, in Isa. 55:1, 'Buy wine and milk,' he says. 'But I have nothing with which to buy, and these things have a price.' Indeed they do, but take them 'without money and without price.' 'But he only calls on those who are thirsty' (verse 1). Yes, that is true, but he refers to a thirst of poverty and total want, not a thirst of spiritual desires. Those who have a spiritual thirst have already tasted this wine and milk and are already blessed (Matt. 5:6). We may even go one step further. In Proverbs 9:4, 5, Christ invites those who 'have no heart' to take of his bread and wine.[4] Usually, this is the last objection that an unbelieving heart makes against itself: it has no mind for Christ. He truly has no heart for Christ. 'Yet,' says Christ, 'this will not get you off. I will not allow this as an excuse. You who have no heart, "turn in here."'

This overriding of all objections by unexpected statements of love, mercy and compassion in the promises is a strong inducement to steadfastness in believing. When a sinner discovers that God takes for granted that everything which he accuses himself of is true; that his sin, folly, heartlessness is just as he has realised, in fact inconceivably worse than he can imagine; that God takes for granted all the aggravations of our sins that lie so dismally before him; our

---

[4] Owen translates a Hebrew word as 'heart,' which in the KJV and ESV is translated 'sense.'

backslidings, perversity, great sin, impotence and coldness, not responding in our affections to the convictions that lie upon us; yet, for all this, he says, 'Come, let us agree. Accept peace, draw near to Christ, receive him from my love,' this must surely encourage us in some measure to rest in, and assent to, the word of promise.

(ii) The second part of this motive may be taken from the *suitability of the promises* for our most urgent needs, troubles, anxieties and fears. What I mean is that though we are exercised with a great variety of doubts and fears, of pressures and perplexities, God has moderated his love and mercy, as offered in the promises, to every one of these needs and difficulties. Had God only revealed himself to us as God almighty, God all-sufficient, he might justly require and expect that we should have faith in him in every situation. But, over and above this, he has, as it were, drawn out his own all-sufficiency in Christ into innumerable streams, flowing to us in all our particular wants, distresses and temptations. When God gave manna in the wilderness it was to be gathered, ground in hand-mills or beaten in mortars, and boiled in pots before it could be eaten (Num. 11:8), but the bread which came down from heaven, the manna in the promises, is already ground, beaten, boiled, ready for everyone's hunger. It is useful to have a well near your house, to which you may go to draw water, but when you have several pipes from a fountain carrying water to every room, it is your own fault if all your needs for water are not supplied. We not only have a well of salvation from which to draw water but innumerable streams also flowing from that well into every empty vessel.

I shall give one or two examples of this kind:

Isaiah 32:2: We are told here that we may be exposed to four pressures and troubles:

(a) the *wind*;

(b) the *storm*,

(c) *drought*,

(d) *weariness*.

To all of these the man in the promise ('a man shall be as an hiding place,' KJV) – the Lord Jesus Christ, the 'king that reigns in righteousness' – is the answer.

(a) The first evil mentioned is the *wind*, and for this Christ is *'a hiding place.'* Someone about to be blown off a high rock by strong winds would look firstly for a hiding place until the strong blasts were over. When fierce winds have cut a ship at sea from all its anchors so that it has nothing to keep it from being dashed upon the rocks, the only hope of the crew is to find a safe harbour, a hiding place. Our Saviour tells us what this wind is (Matt. 7:25). The wind that blows and casts down false professors is the wind of strong and urgent temptations. Is this the state of your soul? Do strong temptations beat upon it, ready to hurry you down into sin and folly? Do you have no rest from them; one blast following after another, so that your soul begins to be faint, to be weary, to give up and say, 'I shall perish. I cannot hold out to the end'? Is this your condition? Then see in this promise how Christ is suited to help you, he is your relief, he is your hiding place. He says, 'These temptations seek your life, but with me you shall be safe.' Fly to him, run to his arms, expect relief from him, and you will be safe.

(b) There is a *storm*, for which Christ is said to be '*a shelter*.' A storm, or tempest, in Scripture, represents the wrath of God because of sin. 'He crushes me with a tempest,' said Job (Job 9:17), when he lay under a sense of the anger and indignation of God. God threatens to rain upon the wicked 'a horrible tempest' (Psa. 11:6, KJV). A tempest is a violent mixture of wind, rain, hail, thunder and darkness. Those who have been at sea can tell you what a tempest means. Such was the case in Egypt (Exod. 9:23). There was thunder and hail, fire running along the ground; fire or dreadful lightning mingled with hail (verse 24). How did men react when warned of this storm? They hurried their servants and cattle into the houses (verse 20), they found a safe place for them that they might not be destroyed, and in this way they were saved.

Imagine a poor creature caught in such a storm, full of sad and dreadful thoughts and fears of the wrath of God. Behind him, before him, around him, he cannot see anything but hailstones and coals of fire. Heaven is dark and dismal above him. He has not seen sun, moon or stars for many days, not one glimpse of light from above or hopes of an end. 'I shall perish; the earth shakes beneath me; the pit is opening for me. Is there no hope?' Now see how Christ is suited for this distress also. He is a shelter from this storm. Get into him and you will be safe. He has borne all this storm as far as you are concerned. Dwell in him and not one hurtful drop shall fall upon you, not one hair of your head shall be singed by this fire. Are you afraid? Do you have a sense of the wrath of God for sin? Do you fear it will one day fall upon you, and be your part? Look, a shelter, a sure defence, provided for you here.

(c) There is *drought* which causes barrenness and makes the heart a dry place, as a heath or a parched wilderness. For this, Christ is as *'streams of water,'* providing abundant streams of refreshment. Drought in the Scripture denotes all kinds of evil, being the great distressing punishment of those countries. When God threatens sinners, he says that they shall be 'like a shrub in the desert, and shall not see any good come' (Jer. 17:6). They shall be left to barrenness and lack of all refreshment. And David complains, in his great distress, that his 'strength was dried up as by the heat of summer' (Psa. 32:4).

Two things are true of this drought: lack of grace or moisture to make the soul fruitful; and lack of rain or consolation to make it joyful. Barrenness and sorrow are the results of such a dry place. Let us then imagine this condition also. Does the soul seem to be as parched ground? It has no moisture to bring forth fruit but is dry and sapless. All the fruits of the Spirit seem to be withered; faith, love, zeal, delight in God, not one of them flourishes. Indeed, it thinks that they are completely dead. It has no showers, no drop of consolation, no refreshment, but pines away under barrenness and sorrow. What would best suit such a condition? Why, turn a stream of water upon this parched ground. Let there be springs in this thirsty place, let 'waters break forth in the wilderness, and streams in the desert' (Isa. 35:6). How all things will be changed! Those things that hung their heads and had no beauty will flourish again; things that are ready to die will be revived. In this condition, Jesus Christ will be water, and water in abundance, rivers of water, so that there will be no want. He will, by his Spirit, give supplies of grace to make the soul fruitful; he will give it much consolation to make it joyful.

(d) There is *weariness*, and in this respect, Christ is said to be '*the shade of a great rock in a weary land.*' Weariness of travel and labour through heat and drought is unendurable. Anyone who has to travel in a thirsty land, dry and hungry, with the sun beating down on his head, will be ready with Jonah to wish he were dead, to be freed of his misery. Oh, how welcome would be 'the shade of a great rock' to such a poor creature! If Jonah rejoiced in the shade of his plant, how much better is the shade of a great rock! Many poor souls, exercised by temptations, hindered in duties, scorched with a sense of sin, are weary in their journey towards Canaan, in their course of obedience. They think to themselves that it might even be better to die than to live, having no hopes of arriving at journey's end. Let such poor souls now lie down and rest a little under the shadow and safe-guarding protection of the Rock of ages, the Lord Jesus Christ. How swiftly will strength and resolution return to them again!

In this way, I say, is Christ in the promises particularly suited to all the various distresses into which we may fall at any time. I might multiply examples to demonstrate this, but this one example should be sufficient to prove the statement that the suitability of the grace revealed in the promises for answering all our needs, should encourage us to believe.

Finally, then, two things may be deduced:

1. *The willingness of God that we should be established in believing.* Why should God override all the objections that

can arise in a doubting heart, and provide Christ with sufficient grace for all the perplexities and troubles that we lie
under at any time, if he was not willing that we should grasp
hold of that grace; own it, accept it, and give him praise for
it? If I should go to a poor man and tell him, 'You are poor,
but look, here are riches; you are naked, but here is clothing;
you are hungry and thirsty, here is food and refreshment;
you are wounded, but I have the most precious balm in
the world,' and if I had no intention of giving him riches,
food, clothing or medicine, wouldn't I be wickedly mocking
and deriding the poor man's misery and sorrow? Would a
wise or good man do that? Though many would deafen
their ears to the cries of the poor, yet who is so desperately
wicked as to enjoy himself by laughing at their misery and
increasing their sorrow? And shall we think that the God
of heaven, 'the Father of mercies and God of all comfort'
(2 Cor. 1:3), who is all goodness, sweetness and truth, when
he so suits and shapes his fullness to our needs, and suits
his grace in Christ for removing all our fears and troubles,
does so purely in order to increase our misery and mock
our calamity? I am speaking of the heirs of the promise,
those to whom they are made, and to whom they belong.
Isn't it time for you to stop disputing and questioning the
sincerity and faithfulness of God in all these engagements
with us? What further, what greater, security can we expect
or wish for?

2. *All unbelief, at last, must be seen to be totally due to
stubbornness of will.* 'You refuse to come to me that you
may have life' (John 5:40). When all a man's objections are
explained and answered, when all his needs are met, when a
basis is laid for all his fears to be removed, and yet he keeps

away and does not draw near; what can that be due to other than the pure perversity of will that rules him? Isn't this kind of person saying, 'Let the Lord do what he wants, say what he wants. Though my mouth is stopped so that I no longer have anything with which to argue back or dispute, yet I will not believe'? Let this, then, be another motive and encouragement, which, when added to all that I have said, concerning God, the Father, and the Lord Jesus Christ, is my main message to you.

Sermon 3

Gospel Love[1]

And above all these put on love, which binds everything to-
gether in perfect harmony.—Col. 3:14

THE word *agape*, which is here translated 'charity,'[2] is the
only word used in the New Testament to signify 'love.' I wish
that it had been translated throughout as 'love,' because in
our everyday use of the word, 'charity' refers only to one
aspect of love: the relieving of the poor and the afflicted.
It is never used in this sense in Scripture. It is 'love,' therefore, that is intended. 'Above all these put on love.' In the
Scriptures the exercising and practising of all the graces and
duties are commanded. Most of them fall under particular
commands which require them absolutely, but this is the
only one, as far as I remember, which is placed in priority
above the others. We see this here: '*Above all these things*
put on love.' And also in 1 Peter 4:8, '*Above all*, keep loving
one another earnestly.'

We see also in 1 Corinthians 12:31 how the apostle had
previously given directions about the use and improvement

---

[1] Preached on 5 June, 1673.
[2] Owen is referring to the KJV rendering of *agape*.

of spiritual gifts for the edification of the church (and there is no better way to edify the church than by the appropriate and orderly exercise of the gifts of the Holy Spirit in the elders and members). But having done this, he adds, 'I will show you a still more excellent way.' That way is this duty of love, as he describes in the following chapter. It is not only commanded but has special priority and excellence placed upon it, above all other duties, for a definite purpose.

What I shall discuss presently is the following:

Observation

Love, together with its exercise, is the principal grace and duty that is required among, and expected from, the saints of God, especially as they are engaged in church-fellowship.

I shall not prove this in general, but speak of three things:

I. I will show you the nature of this love that is emphasized so much in the gospel precept.

II. I will give you reasons for the necessity and importance of it, by noting the reasons the Scriptures give.

III. I will lay down some directions for its good practice.

I. *The love here intended is the second great duty that is brought to light by the gospel.*

It is not found in the world, neither in degree nor as to any knowledge of it, except for that which proceeds from the gospel. The world does not have it nor knows what it is. Disagreement, strife and wrath entered by sin; for when we fell away from the love of God and from his love to us, it is no wonder that we also fell into every hatred and disagreement amongst ourselves. Originally, in the state of innocence, the love of God was the bond of perfect harmony. When

[62]

that was broken, all creation fell into disorder. Mankind, in particular, fell into that state described by the apostle: 'passing our days in malice and envy, hated by others and hating one another' (Titus 3:3). There is still a carnal and natural love in the world, a product of natural relations; it is found, to a lesser degree, even in the animal world. There is also a love that arises from society in sin and in pleasure; from an appropriate humour in conversation, or intrigue in political designs. All the love in the world may be reduced to such means. But these are all utter strangers to evangelical love. Therefore, when it was brought to light by the gospel, there was nothing that amazed the heathen world more than to see this new love practised by Christians. It even became a proverb among them, 'See how they love one another!' To see people of such different kinds, different nations, tempers, degrees, high and low, rich and poor, knit together in love, was the great thing that amazed the heathen world. And I will show you later the source of it.

You may similarly note that this love is the means of communion between all the members of the mystical body of Christ, just as faith is the instrument of their communion with their head, Jesus Christ. Therefore, the apostle, seven or eight times in his epistles, joins faith and love together as the entire means of the communion and fruitfulness of the mystical body of Christ. In one reference, he so arranges his words to affirm their inviolable, inseparable nature, that you have to break them apart in order to understand his exact meaning. This occurs in Philemon, verse 5: 'Hearing of thy love and faith, which thou hast toward the Lord Jesus, and toward all saints' (KJV). One would think that both the objects relate to both the duties: faith and love towards

Christ, and towards all the saints. But although Christ is the object of our love also, the saints are not the object of our faith, so that you must distribute the words to mean: 'hearing of your faith toward the Lord Jesus Christ, and of your love towards all the saints.' The apostle places the two words together to emphasize how indissoluble they are, how they must go together. Where the one is, there you will find the other; where one is not, neither will the other be found. This love is therefore the life and soul and quickening power of all duties fulfilled among believers towards one another. Whatever duties you perform, however great and glorious, however useful to any of the members of Christ, if they are not quickened and animated by this love they are of no value to your communion with Christ, or to the edification of the church. Men may do many things that appear to be duties of love, without love. In the two verses before the text, Paul says, 'Put on then, as God's chosen ones, holy and beloved, humility, meekness and patience, bearing with one another and, if one has a complaint against another, forgiving each other; as the Lord has forgiven you, so you also must forgive. And above all these put on love.' That is, all these things may be done, yet without love. Duties which seem to be the greatest and most effective of all the fruits of love, yet all performed without love. We may forebear without love, forgive without love, be kind to one another without love; and all this would be of no use if, above all these, over and upon them, we do not superimpose love – if we are not quickened and acted upon by love.

The truth is that anyone who reads through the New Testament, especially the reading of those things which we have most reason to consider in it (those things in it which are of greatest importance, namely, the special instructions and commands that Christ left to his disciples when he was about to depart from this world) would think that this love, whatever it might be, is the sum and substance of all that Christ requires of us. And this, of course, is true. The apostle John in his old age, having lived to see the Christian religion spread widely in the world and, very probably, seen a decay of love, wrote his First Epistle with this main purpose: to let us know that there is neither truth of grace, nor evidence of the love of God to us, nor of our love to God, unless there is fervent and intense love towards brothers and sisters. Whatever we may think of our Christian profession, if there is not in us an intense love to the brothers, we have neither the truth of grace, nor evidence of God's love to us, nor of our love to God.

You will therefore say, 'What is this love?'

To answer briefly: It is a fruit of the Spirit of God, an effect of faith, by which believers being knit together by the strongest bonds of affection, stemming from their interest in their one head, Jesus Christ, and participating of one Spirit, delight in, value, and esteem one another, and are constantly ready to fulfil those regular duties by which the temporal, spiritual and eternal good of one another may be promoted.

I will expand this description a little by noting:

1. *This love of which I speak is a fruit of the Spirit, 'the fruit of the Spirit is love' (Gal. 5:22).* There may be, and is, implanted in some natures a great deal of love, kindness and tenderness, compared to others who are difficult to deal with, but that is not the love that is being referred to here. What

specifically produces gospel love is the fact that it is the work of the Holy Spirit in our hearts. I cannot now turn aside to show in detail how we may know whether any expression of love is a fruit of the Spirit or a result of our own natural inclination. You must judge it according to those general rules that are given to discern and distinguish such things. I only emphasize that gospel love must be a fruit of the Spirit, a product of the Holy Ghost in us, otherwise it does not belong to our work.

2. *It is an effect of faith.* According to the apostle, 'Faith [works] through love' (Gal. 5:6). But how does faith work through love? How does faith set love to work? When it has respect to God's command requiring this love; to his promise to accept it; and to his glory, towards which this love is directed. In this way, faith works through love. And if it is not a love which is based on the knowledge that Christ commands it, that he promises to accept it, and that it tends to his glory, then it is not that love for which we aim, towards which we work, and which we press upon you. Self may work through love sometimes; flesh, self-interest or reputation may work through love; that is, through its fruit. But we are referring solely to that love which faith works.

3. *It is that love which knits together the hearts and souls of believers with complete affection towards one another.*

Paul, writing of that communion which the church has by love, tells us of 'the whole body fitly joined together and compacted by that which every joint supplieth' (Eph. 4:16, kjv). We cannot supply anything to one another but by love; delight and esteem flow from love. 'As for the saints in the land,' says the psalmist, 'they are the excellent ones, in whom is all my delight' (Psa. 16:3). We judge that we ought to lay down our lives for our brothers and sisters; that is, to be willing to expose ourselves to difficulties and dangers, to put our lives at risk, even to lay them down, if the edification of the church requires it. The martyrs of old did not lay down their lives only for Christ personally, but for Christ mystical. That is, they not only laid them down in faith, but also in love: love to the church. The apostle says of all his sufferings, 'I am filling up what is lacking in Christ's afflictions for the sake of his body, that is, the church' (Col. 1:24). He bore his afflictions out of love to the church, as well as out of faith and love to Christ personally, so that no offence, scandal or temptation might befall the church. One great reason why the martyrs laid down their lives was that the faith of the church might be confirmed and strengthened. This should be true of us, if ever we are called to it. This is the love of which the Scripture speaks, and not that careless, negligent, carnally-influenced love which the world … (I almost said … No, I will say it) … which too many believers are full of, but of nothing more. It would require not one sermon, but many, to show all the duties that Christ's love requires of us and will move us to perform; how it will influence all our behaviour and direct us in all our ways, in our whole life and conversation, and in all that we do.

In that all believers are to be the objects of this love, it may be asked, 'How are we to exercise it towards them, since there are only a few whom we know or are acquainted with sufficiently to be satisfied that they truly are believers? And only a few of whom we know their circumstances, problems and needs?'

I would answer:

(i) As the whole mystical body of Christ is the object of gospel love, of love in and by the Holy Spirit, it is necessarily required of us that we must have, radically and constantly, an equal love to all believers, as such – to all the followers of Christ throughout the world. But this statement has to be qualified:

(a) The exercise of it will greatly depend on the evidence that people are truly a part of the mystical body of Christ. There are some whose empty opinions and, indeed, corrupt practices, would exercise the most extensive charity before any judgment could be made that they belong to Christ's body; yet, according to our evidence, so is our love to be.

(b) There may be degrees in our love, especially with respect to our delight and esteem, according to whether we see more or less of the image of Jesus Christ upon a believer, in that the likeness and image of Christ is the formal reason for this love.

(c) The exercise of love is determined by circumstances and opportunities.

With these three qualifications, a man may judge that someone is not a believer if he does not, constantly and radically, love all believers in the world, to the extent that he is concerned for their good, and moved to prayer, compassion, delight and joy, according to their various states and conditions.

(ii) An inclination and readiness to act with love towards all believers is required, as opportunities afford. If we turn our face away from our brother and hide ourselves from him, how does God's love dwell in us? If there is anything of this real love in us, and if it is increased and facilitated by opportunity, it will break through difficulties, through arguments, through the pleas of flesh and blood, in order to express itself. Those who know anything in this world realise that, just as the first great opposition of hell, the world and corrupt nature is against faith to God by Christ, so also the next great opposition made against us is against our love. If we do not understand this we are foolish, and have not understood the various states and conditions in this world, and how that, every moment, things are presented to us with the tendency to weaken love, for one reason or another.

(iii) But our Lord Jesus Christ, in infinite wisdom, tenderness and condescension, has provided for us a safe, suitable, constant and immediate object for exercising this love. Having given so great a command for us to love one another, and having laid so much weight upon it, he would not leave us in uncertainty as to how, or where, or when we should exercise it. Accordingly, he has directed us to a particular way in which he will test our obedience to the general rule. He did so by his institution of individual churches. Christ had two great purposes in instituting particular churches: namely, that they might be the means for us to express the two great graces and duties that he requires of us.

(a) The first purpose was that his saints together might jointly profess their faith in him and their obedience to him. And we have no other way of doing it; he has tied us to this way. A blessed way! 'You shall jointly profess your faith in me, and obedience to me, in this way,' he says, 'or not at all.'

(b) The second purpose for instituting a particular church was that we might exercise his other great command, and our other great duty: love to believers. 'I will test you here,' said Christ; 'I require it, of necessity, that you love all the saints, all believers, all my disciples. You will not have to say that you shall have to travel far, in this direction or the other, for objects to love, for I will appoint for you an institution in which you will find continual, immediate objects of that love which I require of you.' When God gives general commands of great consequence, he gives some particular instances in which he will try our obedience to those commands. When he gave that first great command, in the state of innocence, he tested Adam and Eve by the tree of knowledge of good and evil, and by the tree of life. The Lord Jesus Christ has given us this great command of love, and has declared plainly that if we do not love one another we are not his disciples. 'I will provide for you the context in which you will be tested,' he says, 'I will place you in such a society, by my order and appointment, in which you will find immediate objects for the exercise of your love to the utmost that I require.' If we come across an individual who has been properly admitted into church society, he is as certain and evident an object of our love as if we saw him lying in the arms of Christ. We walk by rule; he has appointed us to do so. Let no one then pretend that they love their brothers and sisters, in general, and love the people of God, and love the saints, while their love is not fervently exercised towards those who are in the same church society as themselves. Christ has given it to you as a test; he will try your love at the last day according to your behaviour in the church of which you are a member. The apostle tells us, 'He who does not love his brother whom he has seen cannot love God whom he has not seen' (1 John 4:20). I am sure that I can say that he who does not exercise love towards the brethren whom he has seen, in that relationship in which Christ has appointed him to exercise love, does not love the brethren whom he does not see, and with whom he does not have that particular relationship and acquaintance.

The great Lord and Guide of his church binds this upon the spirits and consciences of us all. It is our life and our being. I declare to this congregation today, I witness and testify to you, that unless this evangelical love is found to be exercised, not loosely and generally, but mutually towards one another among us, we shall never give our account with joy to Jesus Christ, nor shall we ever carry on the great work of edification among ourselves. And if God is pleased to give this spirit among you, I have nothing to fear but the weakness and depravity of my own heart and spirit. This is the great way that Christ has given to us to demonstrate our obedience to that holy command of love to his disciples, and great emphasis is laid upon this duty.

II. *Next I will show you the great reasons why this love is so necessary.*

'Above all these put on love.' 'I will show you a still more excellent way.' We would never come to an end if I insisted on listing all the grounds and reasons for this duty. I will give you some of the ones that seem most important to me. But always remember this, that what I am saying about love is to be exercised, first among yourselves, and then among the whole mystical body of Christ throughout the world, whenever you have opportunity and occasion.

1. *It is necessary because it is the great way by which we testify to the power of the gospel and to our witness to the Messiah, the Christ that was sent by God.* The great work we are to do in this world is to bear witness to the fact that God sent Christ into the world to do the work for which he came. How shall we do this? He tells us himself. 'That they may all be one, just as you, Father, are in me, and I in you, that they also may be in us, so that the world may believe that you have sent me' (John 17:21). Or again: 'I in them and you in me, that they may become perfectly one, so that the world may know that you sent me' (verse 23). This is Christ's emphasis: that the world may be convinced that God has sent him. What will be the evidence for this? He says: 'If all believers are one, that will be the evidence.' I acknowledge that there is another principle of oneness among those who believe, namely the participation in that one Spirit of the Father and of the Son, by which we become one in the Father and the Son. But that is not the whole of our oneness. In fact, I do not think it is the oneness referred to here at all. My reason is that this second unity in the Spirit is perfectly invisible and imperceptible to the world. But Christ prays for such a unity that will convince the world; that the world will see that we are one and so believe that God had sent him. The only unity that will convince the world that God has sent Christ is that which is bound together in the perfect harmony of love, that for which love is its life, soul and spirit. And if this love is not eminent in us we are only contributing to what hardens the world in its unbelief. Persons who profess the gospel, to a greater or lesser extent, have manufactured a unity and uniformity for themselves, but by neglecting this unity of love for the

sake of mere outward unity they have become the greatest means for hardening the world in unbelief. 'There is nothing remarkable here,' says the world. 'I could make such a union as this whenever I felt like it. It only involves drawing up a set of rules about outward observances and ensuring that people keep them.' But only Jesus Christ can bring about a true union of love.

And why will it convince the world that God has sent Christ, when disciples do love one another in this way? What forms the argument? What is the basis for seeking to prove that God has sent his Son on the grounds that his disciples love one another in this way? It lies in what I have already mentioned: when sin entered, the bond of all union and perfection among creatures was completely broken, because love was lost. The whole was irrecoverably delivered to envy, wrath, 'hated by others and hating one another.' Nothing under heaven, no human resource, could retrieve mankind so as to love again with pure spiritual love. God sent Christ to retrieve this loss, to bring in a new creation, to bring things to order, to renew the world and the face of things. That glorious part of this work which is wrought in the heart of man is invisible; that which is visible is love. The world sees in Christ's disciples a new unity, one that is not in the world, nor of the world; one that the world cannot be part of. By this they know that God has sent Christ to do this great work. The care, kindness, graciousness, love, delight and concern that we have for one another, as members of the mystical body of Christ, exemplified in our unique church relationships, is the great testimony to the world that God has sent Christ. And they will be forced to see and say at last, 'A glorious work has been done to these people. They were once "foolish, disobedient, led astray, slaves to various passions and pleasures, passing their days in malice and envy, hated by others and hating one another," but a glorious work has been done by the Son in them. And we acknowledge that this is from Christ, from God having sent him for this reason and purpose.'

2. *This love is necessary because without it we have no evidence that we ourselves are Christ's disciples.* 'A new commandment I give to you, that you love one another: just as I have loved you, you also are to love one another. By this all people will know that you are my disciples, if you have love for one another' (John 13:34, 35). Why is it that this command of love here, and in other places, is called a new commandment? I mentioned before that when sin entered the world, envy and hatred entered with it, and have continued for the same reason. 'What causes quarrels and what causes fights among you?' asks the apostle. 'Is it not this, that your passions are at war within you?' (James 4:1). In the first revelation that God gave of himself in the law, he commanded love. Our Lord Jesus Christ tells us this: that we are commanded to 'love the Lord your God with all your heart [and] your neighbour as yourself.' Why, then, is this command so often called a new commandment? 'A new commandment I give to you, that you love one another,' he said.

There are various reasons for this:

(i) I think that one reason may be that under the law God indulged that carnal people in many things in which they were short of the royal law of love, because of the hardness of their hearts. When Christ came and delivered this command to its full extent, it came as a new commandment.

(ii) They were carnal and did not see the spirituality of the command. And the truth is that you hear so little of it in the Old Testament, and so much of it in the New Testament, that Christ may justly call it a new commandment.

(iii) At the time of Christ's coming, destructive expositions of the law existed. These were current throughout the church and had overthrown the whole duty of love between its brothers, sisters and members. We find the Saviour having to vindicate this duty (Matt. 5). But in that he came to end all indulgence to carnal men because of the hardness of their hearts, to take away the darkness that was upon their minds, hiding from them the spirituality of the command, and to remove those false expositions of the law, he called it a new commandment.

(iv) There is one further reason, above all, lying in this text that I have just read to you: 'A new commandment I give to you, that you love one another: just as I have loved you, you also are to love one another.' The reason why it was a new commandment was that there was no quickening, enlivening example of it, expressing the power of love, to be found in the Old Testament. This was reserved for Christ. He comes and gives that glorious example of love in his condescension in all that he did and all that he suffered. He shows that there is something in love of which they had never previously had an example. It is because of this that the command to love is expressed as: 'Let this mind be in you, which was also in Christ Jesus' (Phil. 2:5, KJV); 'Love one another, as I have loved you.' In this way it is a new commandment indeed, such as it never was before. 'In this way,' says Christ, 'men will know that you are my disciples: in that the great example that I have set before you, the great command that I have given you, and the great work which I came into the world to perform, was to renew love. It is by love that men will know that you are my disciples and by nothing else.' We have no other way of proving ourselves to be his followers. Men's abilities, gifts, wisdom, will not do it. If there is no love, the world has no reason to conclude that we are followers of Jesus Christ.

3. *Love is necessary because it is the main element of the communion of saints.* There is much talk about the saints' communion. And it is certainly a great thing. We note that it had a place in all the ancient creeds of the church. These profess belief in God, in Christ, and in the Holy Spirit; and they also profess belief in the communion of saints, showing it to be of great importance.

What does it consist of? There are three things in it:

(i) Its fountain and spring;

(ii) Its profession and expression; and

(iii) Its formal reason and life.

(i) The fountain and spring of the communion of saints lies in their common participation in one Spirit from the one head, Jesus Christ. To establish a communion among professors which is not based on a common participation in the same Spirit with Christ as head, would be like trying to form a social group made up of dead men.

(ii) Its expression is seen principally in the participation of the same ordinances in the same church. This is the great manifestation of the communion of saints.

(iii) The life and formal reason of this communion, which derives strength from its fountain, and communicates itself in its expression, lies in love.

I have truly a great concern of spirit that churches have been apt to define their communion too much, if not solely, in their participation in the same ordinances, depending on the same pastor or teacher: joining together in the celebration of the same sacred institutions. Friends, this is only the expression of our communion. There may be a communion in the ordinances without any communion of saints. You know how much of this exists in the world. If we are not acted upon and influenced by this love in all that we do, there is no communion. The extent of your faithfulness to your station in the church of God, the extent to which you discharge your duty and act as living members of the church, is just that extent to which you find love acting in you towards one another, and no further. Your utmost care in attending to good order, your constant presence at the celebration of the ordinances, your dependence on the doctrine and instruction provided by the church, may all be performed without the communion of saints. These may all be present, but it is love that makes it communion. Love is its life and the formative reason for it, as you may see in the text already quoted (Eph. 4:15, 16): 'Rather, speaking the truth in love, we are to grow up in every way into him who is the head, into Christ, from whom the whole body, joined and held together by every joint with which it is equipped, when each part is working properly, makes the body grow so that it builds itself up in love.'

This text is the greatest and most glorious description of the communion of saints that we have in the Scriptures. It begins with love, 'speaking the truth in love'; and it ends in love, 'it builds itself up in love.' It is also carried on by love. We see here the fountain and source of this communion, that lies in its head, in our relation to, and our dependence upon Christ, the head. If we do not hold onto the head we can have no share in this communion. But it is not enough that there should be a head; there should be a 'growing up in every way into him, who is the head.' We shall never carry on the work of communion unless we grow up into Christ: by direct dependence upon him; by deriving life and strength from him; by returning all things to his praise and glory as our head. In this way we are brought nearer and made more like him. The exercise of faith in these things is how we grow up into Christ.

Suppose, then, that we have advanced to this extent in the business of communion: that we hold the head by faith, and are growing up into the head by the exercise of faith and obedience. What is next? 'From whom the whole body, joined and held together.' There will be such supplies from the head, Christ, whom the members of the body hold and grow up into, that will communicate a variety of gifts and graces which will fit and suit the body, and every member of it to another.

But how are believers placed into church union and order? I will not say how this is *not* done: I know the various attempts made in the world. But I will plainly explain how they *are* so placed. It is by the various communications of

Christ, the head, to them all, fitting and suiting them to one another. What is their part in this? They may be joints or some other parts. They may be joints, that is, officers or leading members who, because of the gifts they have received, communicate the effects of those gifts and graces, spreading abroad the supply provided by the head. What of the other members? Not only the joints but every part, when working properly, contributes to this work. The graces and gifts of Christ assign a place for each member. None of us is to choose our own part in God's house. The graces and gifts given us place us as a part, or joint, and from that position we add our supply according to the measure of our gifts, and no more is required of us. But how shall we do this? Christ tells us, 'speaking the truth in love.' The plain meaning of which is that whatever we do in declaring or obeying the truth – in preaching, or in the path of duty – we do it all in love. It is not merely speaking or declaring but fulfilling whatever we do in obedience to the truth. Whatever your concern with the truths of the gospel, let love be involved in it; it is the means by which you convey your supplies, received from every joint or part, to the whole.

Truth requires our pity, compassion, admonition, exhortation, long-sufferance, and similar responses. 'Do it all in love,' says the apostle. What will be the result? 'The body will grow so that it builds itself up in love.' It is all love. I have sometimes thought that 'in love,' in the original Greek, might be read as 'by love': 'it builds itself up by love.' But if we decide on the first rendering, 'builds itself up in love,' it teaches that love in the body will increase, and that where love is, there the body will be built up. A church full of love is a church well built. I would a thousand times prefer to see a church filled with love than filled with the best, highest and most glorious gifts and abilities that men may possess. Were they to obtain everything that they desired, were they to 'speak in the tongues of men and angels,' it would still be ten thousand times better, for the glory of God and for their own comfort, to be a company of poor sinners who are filled with love, than to be those of the highest attainments without it. We do not testify to the world that God sent Christ, nor provide evidence that we are his disciples, nor contribute anything to the building up of the church, unless God gives us the grace of love abundantly. Whatever our gifts and skills, and whatever our wisdom, these things tend to puff us up. If this love does not abound in us we shall only be thorns in one another's sides, and will not contribute anything to the real spiritual edification of the church. Paul does not only state this but argues it fully in the twelfth and thirteenth chapters of the First Epistle to the Corinthians so that there is no need for me to dwell on it. 'If I speak in the tongues of men and of angels, but have not love, I am a noisy gong or a clanging cymbal,' that makes a little pleasant sound which comes to nothing. I would conclude every argument with the following: If we do not have love, we do not have grace. 'Everyone who loves the Father loves whoever has been born of him' (1 John 5:1). If we do not love the brethren the love of God does not dwell in us. Our external order and form, our duties, or anything that we do, will provide no evidence that we possess anything of the grace of God if we do not have this grace of love.

III. *Having spoken so much on the nature of evangelical love and of the reasons for its importance, I wish to say something to impress this upon your hearts and mine.*

The success of our work today to which you have called us, under the care and kindness of Christ, depends completely on this one thing, our fulfilling of this one duty of love. I don't know how it has happened, but it is true that lately believers have been remarkably harassed by sharp accusations and bitter rebukes for their lack of love. I can't see that any good has come from this, or any advantage gained. The reason for it seems to be that behind it lies the belief: 'If you will do so-and-so; if you will follow such-and-such practices in the performance of your religion; if you will go only this far and do this much; if you stop these and those ways which you follow – then you have love. If not, you have none at all.' And what has been the result of all this? New divisions, new animosities, new quarrels and disputes – without the least appearance of any improvement of love whatsoever. I would be very sorry if anyone should desire more than I do that all who fear God throughout the world, especially in these nations, were of one way and procedure as well as of one heart. I know that I desire it sincerely. But I truly believe that when God accomplishes this, it will be the effect of love, and not the cause of love. It will proceed from love before it brings forth love. There is no greater folly in the world, in my poor judgment, than to drive men into a particular way of doing things, and then suppose that love will necessarily be the result: to think that, with harsh accusations and biting, cutting expressions, they have only to force men into particular practices, and then love will inevitably ensue. We see the opposite all the world over: that those who most boast and glory at bringing all to uniformity in practice have the least love among themselves. You see it in the papal church. They have obtained their purpose, in driving all into one uniform church; yet, its members are fighting and tearing one another. It is an empty presumption to believe that men may be brought to some arrangement, whether they want to or not, and that then all will be love, whether they wish it or not.

I truly do not know of any way followed by those who walk in the fear of God (though some might be nearer the truth than others) which is, in itself, an obstacle to love. I testify that if I did I would fly from that way as from a plague-house, or anything else that is mortally destructive, because I know that the purpose of all Christ's institutions is to increase love. Some may be nearer the truth than others; some, indeed are so; but if any way is truly an obstacle to love, I would leave it without further consideration, without debating whether it was right or wrong; because I know it would be wrong. For any person to comment on any institution of Christ (which is what many individual churches are and will be proved to be) as though they were hindrances to love argues either a great ignorance of God's ways or, indeed, an ill-will towards them. On the contrary, they are appointed by God for this purpose, that in them we may first exercise that love towards one another which he commanded so directly, that we might then learn to show it to all believers throughout the world. Do not let us be overtaken by any such thought that we cannot exercise love until we arrive at such and such a particular agreed order, and thereby so put off the duty until such a time when we would have no opportunity or ability to exercise it. Let us address ourselves to it in our present state and condition.

I shall close with two or three cautions against things that may be hindrances in the diligent practice of this great duty of which I have been speaking:

1. *Beware of a morose, sour natural disposition.*

Even if it does not hinder many fruits of love, yet it deeply undermines the glory of its acting. Some good people are so like Nabal that they spoil the sweet fruit of their loving actions. It is soured by an unpleasant disposition that has no life or beauty in it. It is a great mistake to believe that grace merely subdues our carnal corruption rather than changing our natural temper. I believe that grace changes the natural temper and ennobles it. It makes 'the leopard to lie down with the young goat,' and 'the lion to eat straw like the ox,' as was the promise. It makes the irascible meek, the intolerant patient, and the morose gentle and kind. And we are to make use of grace to this end, and not to humour and please ourselves, and act as if these things can never be altered in us. Grace comes to alter our natural dispositions which are incompatible with love and hinder us from acting lovingly. We are too ready to excuse ourselves and others, and hope that Christ will do so also, because this or that action is part of our natural personality. Pray that we should not be like this; our temperament must be cured by grace, otherwise grace is not fulfilling its perfect work in us.

2. *Beware of those hindrances to love which may arise from your particular position or condition.*

I refer to those who have the advantage of riches, wealth, honour or reputation in the world. Such people can be so surrounded by various circumstances that they do not know how to break through them and demonstrate

[83]

that familiarity of love with the poorest member of the church, which is required of them. Brothers, you know that the gospel allows you to enjoy all your providential advantages; whatever you have in terms of birth, education, inheritance, estate, titles or position. But in everything that has respect to our communion together, the gospel renders us all equal; there is neither rich nor poor, slave nor free in Christ, but only the new creature. We are therefore expressly commanded by James that we should give no particular respect in the congregation to any on account of their outward advantages (James 2:1-9). We all serve one common Master, the same Lord; and he is such a Lord, that when he was rich in all the glory of heaven, he became poor for our sakes. Let me beg of those of you who are rich to remember this Lord and Master whom we have in common; do not let your outward privileges, therefore, keep you at a distance from the meanest, poorest saint that belongs to your congregation. If they do, your riches are your temptation, and your status your disadvantage, and you must labour to break through them.

I might also say something to the poorest and lowest among us, who also have their temptations, keeping them from exercising love. But I shall pass that by.

3. *Lastly, beware, all of you, of being satisfied with the duties of love, without looking after the entire working of the grace of love.*

You, here, who are joining with us today, have had for so long a time such a great and wise instructor that I am quite sure that you have been taught all the duties of love required of you in your various relationships and that you practice them fully. I only ask you to make sure that you are found full of the spirit of the grace of love: that which comes from faith and is worked in you by the Holy Spirit. This alone will enable you to delight in, and to esteem and value highly the saints, and will create a cheerfulness and readiness in you for fulfilling all these duties.

I meant to have given you many other directions, but I must end. If God is pleased to impress anything from this word upon your hearts and spirits, we will have cause to rejoice in it. But at least, remember this: that you were begged and exhorted – as you regard the glory of God, the honour of the gospel, and the edification of the church (of which two have now become one), for which you must all in your different situations give an account, as well as I in mine; and as you have any respect towards the ministry of him whom God has set over you – that all might be received within this one duty of love. If God is pleased to increase and intensify this amongst us, I do not doubt that he will prosper today's work of uniting us together.

Sermon 4

Walking Humbly with God

And to walk humbly with your God—Mic. 6:8

THE sixth chapter of Micah begins with a most affecting reproof by God, addressed to his people and delivered by his prophet, with respect to their sins and unworthy walk before him. He first stirs up their attention by means of an exclamatory passage addressed to the mountains and hills (verses 1, 2). Then he calls on them to take notice of his complaint against them and presses upon them the mercies that he had bestowed on them in the past, and the patience and love with which he had dealt with them (verses 3–5).

This message having been effective in waking them and filling them with a sense of their awful ingratitude and rebellion (verses 6, 7), the people (as is usual in those under the power of conviction) begin to ask what steps they must take to avoid God's wrath, which they acknowledged they truly deserve. And now, as is often the case when God speaks with the intention of healing his people (see Hos. 7:1), their iniquity and wickedness are increasingly revealed to them. They discover the wretched principles upon which they have acted in all their dealings with God.

It is generally the case that when conviction lays hold on the soul, by whatever means, it discloses the soul's inward principles in a way that is not otherwise experienced. There are many who have, in their minds, received the doctrine of free justification by the blood of Christ and, as a consequence, are complacent and secure in their ways, without trouble and distress. It is impossible to persuade these that they do not live and act upon that principle, and do not walk before God in its strength. But if some great conviction from the word or from some pressing danger or trouble falls upon them, then their hearts are laid open, and it is found that all their hopes are based on their own repentance, on their moral improvement, on the increased performance of duties. And the iniquity of their self-righteousness is revealed.

This was how it was with the Jews. Having been indicted of their sins by the prophet so that they were not able to stand under such a weight and burden, he now reveals to them the ground of all their dealings with God, namely, that having provoked him, they were now seeking what they could do in order to appease him and to atone his anger.

In their plans, to this end, they decide on two approaches:

Firstly, they suggest things that God himself had appointed for them to do (verses 6, 7). Secondly, they suggest things of their own invention which, they supposed, might have a further and better effect than anything that God had appointed (verse 7).

In this way, they first look to sacrifices and burnt offerings for help: they consider whether, on their account, they might come before the Lord and bow themselves before the high God. That is, they debate the nature of the worship they might perform by which they might be acquitted from the guilt of their sins.

Sacrifices were part of the worship of God that he himself had appointed; they were acceptable to him provided they were offered in faith and according to his mind. Yet, in the Old Testament, we frequently find God rejecting sacrifices, even when they were still in force and conformed to his instruction. This rejection was not absolute but had respect to aspects that disqualified the service offered by them. Among these aspects were two in particular:

1. When they were viewed and trusted as the cause of justification and acceptance with God, in and of themselves, rather than in their function as types.

2. When they were relied on to gain God's approval by men who were neglecting their moral duties or continuing in sinful ways.

Both these evils were involved in this appeal of the Jews to their sacrifices. Their appeal was firstly in order to please God, or to appease him – that by them they might be freed from the guilt of sin and be accepted – but also that they then might be accepted by God in their continuing immoralities and wickedness. This is evident from the reply of the prophet (verses 7, 8), as he calls them from their vain confidence in sacrifices, to justice, judgment, mercy and a humble walk with God.

They then, secondly, found that this was not enough. Their consciences were not satisfied, nor peace obtained, by any performance of these ordinary duties, even if they were to be carried out in an extraordinary manner: bringing 'thousands of rams' and 'ten thousand rivers of oil.' Though men, terrified by the guilt of sin, attempt in the most vigorous and extraordinary way to quieten their souls by all appointed duties, they never succeed. The work is never accomplished, and so they take further steps. If nothing that God has appointed for them will bring peace to their souls (because they were not appointed by God for that purpose) they will invent, or make use of, methods of their own that they believe may be of greater efficacy than the first: 'Shall I give my firstborn for my transgression?'

The rise and occasion of the kind of sacrificing mentioned here – the sacrifice of men; of children by their parents; its use throughout the world and among all nations; the craft and cruelty of Satan in imposing them on poor, sinful, guilty creatures, and the advantages he had to do this – I have described elsewhere. I shall presently note two things only of the state and condition of convicted people, pressed by their sins and by a sense of the guilt of their sins, yet ignorant of the righteousness of God in Christ:

1. *They have a better opinion of their own ways and efforts to please God and quieten their consciences than of anything instituted by God or laid down by him for that purpose.* This is the height to which they rise, once they have determined on that which is most glorious in their own eyes. Tell a Papist who is under conviction of sin of the blood of Christ – it is folly to him. Penances, satisfaction, purgatory, the intercession of the church in the mass: these seem so much more desirable to him. These Eliabs must wear the crown (see 1 Sam. 16:6). Innumerable poor sinners are presently in the same situation, hoping to find greater relief in appeasing God and obtaining peace from their own duties and improvements of life than from the blood of Christ.

2. *There is nothing so horrid, desperate, oppressive or wicked that convicted people will not do under the pressure of guilt for sin.* They will burn their children in the fire, the cries of their conscience being louder than the wails of their poor infants. They demonstrate both the desperate blindness that is man's by nature, that he should choose such abominations rather than that way which is the wisdom of God, and the desperate terrors that possess poor souls convinced of sin and unaware of the only remedy.

To these poor creatures, in their state and condition, the prophet reveals their mistake and desperate folly in the words of my text.

Two things are contained in the verse: one is implied, the other expressed directly.

(1) That which is implied is the reproof of the error and mistake of the Jews. They thought that sacrifices were appointed so that God might be appeased by them, and that this was the required nature of worship; that their duty in performing sacrifices made satisfaction for the guilt of sin. Micah calls them from this, telling them that this is not their duty, not their business. God has provided another way to make reconciliation and atonement. It is something far above their power. Their business is to walk with God in holiness. As far as atonement is concerned, that is an entirely different matter. 'He has told you, O man, what is good, and what…the Lord requires of you.' He does not expect satisfaction at your hands, but obedience on the basis of peace that has already been made.

(ii) What is expressed directly is this: that God prefers moral worship, offered obediently, to all sacrifices whatever, according to that standard later approved by our Saviour (Mark 12:33): 'What the Lord requires of you.'

He relates this moral obedience to three things: doing justly; loving mercy; walking humbly with God.

The first two of these duties include the whole of our duty with respect to men; they contain the sum and substance of the second table of the law. I do not intend to deal further with these.

The third head is what I wish to concentrate on; it speaks particularly of the first table and the moral duties required by it. I shall mention three things:

I. What it is to walk with God (the remainder of this sermon, together with Sermon 5, pp. 103-117);

II. What it is to walk humbly with God (Sermon 6, pp. 119-136 and Sermon 7, pp. 137-152);

III. The proof of these propositions (Sermon 8, (pp. 153-169). Humble walking with God, as our God in covenant, is the great duty and most precious concern of believers.

I. *What it is to walk with God.*

We must learn what is required beforehand in order for this to be fulfilled, and, secondly, what is required in its performance, what is its nature.

1. *Some things are required before we can walk with God,* such as:

(i) *Peace and agreement.* 'Do two walk together, unless they have agreed to meet?' (Amos 3:3). And Amos adds that walking with God, when there is no peace with him, is like walking in a forest where a lion is roaring (verse 8), when a man can think of nothing else but the fear of being immediately torn to pieces and eaten. It is in this way that God threatens to deal with those who pretend to walk with him, but yet are not at peace with him: 'Mark this, then, you who forget God, lest I tear you apart, and there be none to deliver!' (Psa. 50:22). Who are these people? They are those to whom he speaks in verse 16: 'But to the wicked God says.' The introductory 'But' distinguishes them from those of whom he had been speaking previously in the psalm (verse 5), those who 'had made a covenant with me by sacrifice,' and so obtained peace in the blood of Christ. When Cain and Abel went into the field together and were not agreed, the result was that one killed the other. When Joram met Jehu in the field, he cried, 'Is it peace?' And when, from the answer he received, he found out that they were not agreed, he immediately fled, crying out for his life (2 Kings 9:21-24). '"Agree," says our Saviour, "with thine adversary quickly, whiles thou art in the way with him," lest the outcome be a sad one for you' (Matt. 5:25, KJV).

You know the enmity that exists between God and man, while man is in his natural state, alienated from God by wicked works. They are enemies, for the mind that is set on the flesh is hostile to God (Rom. 8:7), the wrath of God remains on them (John 3:36), they are children of his wrath (Eph. 2:3). If I were to expand on this point, I could show from the occasion of the first disobedience, from considering the parties in dispute, from the various ways in which the rift developed, and from its final result, that this is the saddest enmity that could ever be contemplated. You also know what our peace and agreement with God is, and how that arose. Christ is 'our peace' (Eph. 2:14). He put an end to the division due to sin (Dan. 9:24). He has made peace for us with God, and by our interest in him we who were far off have been brought near and obtain peace (Rom 5:1; Eph. 2:13-15).

This, then, is what is required in the first place if we are to walk with God: that we should be at peace with him, and that there should be agreement in the blood of Christ. That, by faith, we should have a share in the atonement; that our persons should be accepted so that we possess the foundation necessary for the acceptance of our duties. Without this, every attempt at walking with God in obedience, or at the fulfilling any duty, is:

(a) *Fruitless*. All that men do is lost. 'The sacrifice of the wicked is an abomination to the Lord' (Prov. 15:8); their holy things are dung, which God will remove. In all their duties they labour in the fire; none of their works will benefit their eternal account. God looks on all their duties as the gifts of enemies that are selfish, deceitful and, of all things, to be abhorred. Such men may have their reward in this life, but as far as that for which they aim, their pains are lost, their worship is lost, their alms are lost. All is fruitless.

(b) *Presumptuous*. They force themselves into the presence of God; he who hates them and is hated by them. 'But to the wicked God says: "What right have you to recite my statutes or take my covenant on your lips?"' (Psa. 50:16). This is God's language to them as they engage in their duties. 'Why do you howl in this way before me, and offer swine's blood in my presence? How were you able to come here without a wedding garment? I hate your most solemn oblations.' It will be found that at the heart of all the attempts of unregenerate men to walk with God lies an intolerable presumption. They think that it is an easy thing to do; they deal with God as if he was someone who takes very little notice of how he is dealt with.

This, I say, is the first thing required for us to walk with God: that we should be at peace with him and in agreement with him in the blood of Christ. And, as the psalmist says, 'Consider this, you who do not know God,' who have not made a covenant with him, in and by the sacrifice of his Son. You meet with him in the field, you put yourself in his company, you pretend to walk with him in this and that duty, which habit, education, conviction or self-righteousness have taught you. In every one of them you provoke him to his face to destroy you. You seem to flatter him that you are agreed, when in fact he declares that you are at enmity. Let a man deal in this way with his ruler – conspiring against his crown and dignity, attempting his death, despising his authority, reproaching his reputation – and then, after he has been proclaimed a rebel and traitor, and condemned to die, let him come into his presence, as in the past, and act before him as if he were a good subject – offering to him gifts and presents – does he think that he will escape? Won't he, rather, be seized and delivered over to punishment?

Every man in his natural state is a rebel against God. You have rejected his authority, conspired to ruin him, and ruin his kingdom; you have been proclaimed by him a traitor and a rebel, and sentenced to eternal death. Is it right that you now go to meet him, flatter him with your mouth and fawn upon him in your other duties? Won't he remember your rebellions, despise your offerings, command you out of his presence into chains and prison, and abhor your gifts? What else can you expect from his hands? This is the most and best you can expect, in your state, from your actions of obedience, if you have no share in Christ. The more sincere and zealous you are, the readier in the fulfilling of your duties, the more you are presuming upon him and his company; he, who hates you on the most just grounds in the world and is ready to destroy you.

(ii) The second thing required beforehand is *unity of purpose*. People who are only in one another's company now and again, for brief periods, cannot be said to be walking together. This requires unity of purpose and intent.

God's purpose, in general, is his own glory. He makes all things for himself (Prov. 16:4; Rev. 4:11). Our duty of walking with him has the one particular purpose of praising his glorious grace (Eph. 1:6).

Now, in this purpose of God to exalt his glorious grace, two things are important. Firstly, that everything that we desire from God's hand is to be acknowledged as the result of mere grace and mercy (Titus 3:4, 5). God aims at the exalting of his glory by being known, believed and magnified, as a God who pardons iniquity and sin. And secondly, that this enjoyment of himself, in this way of mercy and grace, is the great reward of those who walk with him. God tells Abraham, when he calls him to walk before him, 'I am thy shield, and thy exceeding great reward' (Gen. 15:1, KJV). The enjoyment of God in covenant, and all the good things freely promised and bestowed by him, is the exceeding great reward of those who walk with God. This, then, is necessary for those who wish to walk with God: they must have the same purpose in doing so as God has; they must aim, in all their obedience, at the glory of God's grace, and at the enjoyment of him as their exceeding great reward.

According to what was said before with respect to God's purpose, this involves three things:

(a) In general, the individual's purpose must be the exalting of the glory of God. 'Whatsoever you do,' says the apostle (that is, in our worship of God, and our walk with him), 'do all to the glory of God' (1 Cor. 10:31). Men, who, in their obedience, have base, low, unworthy motives, are as opposed to God in that obedience as in their sins. Some serve him out of habit; some for an increase of corn, wine and oil, or for the satisfying of some low earthly reason; some aim for self and reputation. All is lost: this is not walking with God but warring against him.

(b) Exalting God's grace. This is part of the ministry of the gospel: in our obedience we should aim at exalting the glory of grace. The first natural tendency of obedience was the exalting of the glory of God's justice. The new covenant has provided another purpose for our obedience: that of exalting free grace. Grace given us in Christ, enabling us to obey; grace accepting our obedience, although unworthy; grace constituting this way of walking with God; grace crowning its performance.

(c) Aiming at the enjoyment of God as our reward. This is what disqualifies the obedience of many from being a true walk with God. They do indeed perform duties, but what sincerity is there in their aims for God's glory? Is it something to which they ever give a thought? Isn't the sole aim of their obedience the hope of satisfying their conscience and of an escape from hell and wrath? Is it of any concern to them that God's glory should be exalted? Do they truly care what becomes of his name or ways as long as they are saved? How little, particularly, do they aim for the glory of God's grace! Men are destroyed by self-righteousness and have nothing of gospel obedience in them. Look at the praying and preaching of some men. Isn't it clear that they do not walk with God in this work, do not seek his glory, have no zeal for it and no care for his name? They are fully satisfied with the mere fulfilling of the duty.

(iii) For a man to walk with another it is necessary for him *to be alive*. Dead men cannot walk; or, if they do, acted upon by something other than their own life, they become a terror to their companions, not a comfort in communion. For a dead corpse or carcass to be moved up and down, is not walking. We therefore find that this principle necessary for our obedience is frequently noted in Scripture: that we 'who were dead have been made alive'; that 'the law of the Spirit of life has set you free in Christ Jesus from the law of sin and death' (Rom. 8:2). For us to walk with God, a principle of new life is required. This is what provides us with the power to walk; it urges us from within to walk. Wouldn't a man prefer to be on his own than be accompanied by a dead body, taken out of the grave and manipulated by external forces and powers?

This is the third consideration. Walking with God consists, as I will show, in our obedience, in our performance of the duties required. In this, we are all engaged. Indeed, so much is this so, that it is perhaps hard to discover who walks fastest, with the greatest appearance of strength and life. But alas! How many dead souls we have walking among us!

Are there none among us of those who are utter strangers to new spiritual life – a life from above, hidden with Christ in God, a life of God – that almost mock at such things; or, at least, can give no account of any such life in them? They think it unnecessary that they should be required to testify of any experience of this life, or to witness to being born again by the Spirit. Such a thing would be ridiculous! How then do they defend themselves? 'Why are we not walking with God?' they say. 'Isn't our conversation good and blameless? Who can accuse us of anything? Don't we fulfil the duties required of us?' But, friend, would it be acceptable to you to have a dead man taken out of his grave and carried along with you in your way? This is exactly what all your services and company are to God. He smells only a putrid steam from your presence with him: your hearing, prayers, duties, meditations. They are all, because of this, an abomination to him. Do not talk to me of your behaviour. If it springs from a pure conscience (that is, a conscience purified in the blood of Christ) and sincere faith, which is that life, or the fruit of that life, which we are considering, it is glorious and commendable. If from any other principle, the Lord abhors it.

Are there none among us of those who are motivated in their obedience and duties, not from inward principles and spiritual faculties but merely from outward considerations and external influences? The apostle tells us how believers 'grow' and 'go on to maturity' (Eph. 4:16; Heb. 6:1). Christ is the head; from whom, by the Spirit, every joint and sinew receives that influence of life, so that the body grows and builds itself up. But what about many others? They are set on their feet by habit or by some conviction. One joint is equipped by reputation, another by fear and shame, a third by self-righteousness and a fourth by the lash of conscience. In this way they are driven on by external impressions. These are the principles of obedience for many. It is by things like these that they are motivated in their walk with God. Do you think that you will be accepted? Or that at your final end you will find peace? I fear that many who are listening to me today are in this condition. Forgive me if I am jealous over you with godly jealousy (2 Cor. 11:2, KJV). What other explanation is there for that hatred of the power of the gospel, that darkness in the mystery of the gospel, that cursed formality, that enmity to the Spirit of God, that hatred of reformation, which is found among us?

Application

If there are so many things required for men to be equipped to walk with God, and if there are so many who strive to do so but are yet lost, in the midst of all their obedience and performance of duties, because of some defect in these things, what will become of those who shall be found not to have once attempted to walk with him: those who have never been motivated by any means to make it their business to do so? I am not speaking only of those among us, young and old, whose pride, folly, idleness, loose living, profaneness, hatred of God's ways, testify to their faces and to all the world of the shame and danger of the condition in which they live, that they are servants of sin and walk contrary to God. And God also will walk contrary to them, until they are no more. I repeat, I am not speaking of these, who are judged by all; nor yet only of those who maintain outward observances merely on account of the discipline of their church situation, or the hopes they have laid up in it for their outward good, or for other carnal reasons. But I speak of those also who ought to be the leaders of others, and examples to the flock which is among us. What endeavours to walk with God are found in them, or seen in their ways? Vanity, pride in themselves, in their families and relations, even scoffing at religion and at the ways of God, this is the example that some provide. I hope that worldliness, selfishness, hardness, and lack of love, together with evident vanity, do not undermine all motivations to walk with God amongst others.

The vanity of this highest profession, yet without humble walking, is another deceit of which I shall have much to say later.

For the present, let me speak to those whom I have already addressed. If many shall cry 'Lord, Lord,' and not be heard; if many shall 'strive to enter,' but shall not; what will be their lot and portion? Poor creatures! You do not know the condition of your souls. You cry 'peace,' but 'sudden destruction will come upon you' (1 Thess. 5:3). Beware, lest the many sermons and exhortations you have heard cause you to end up as those who live near the waterfalls of mills and who are deaf to their noise. God sometimes sends his messengers to make men deaf (Isa. 6:10). If that is your situation, it will be sad for you. Allow me to ask you one or two questions.

(i) Are you not used to indulging yourselves, some of you, in your behaviour and in your contempt of others? You think that those who reprove you are fools, or envious, or hypocrites or quarrelsome; and you scorn them in your hearts. You, rather, love, honour and imitate those who have never pressed you (nor ever will) with respect to this business of a new life: of walking with God. From the occasion that this new style of preaching was first heard among you, you believe that the times have been ruined. You long to hear fine speeches and the pretensions of men who are ignorant of God and of themselves.

(ii) Or do you find relief by deceiving yourselves, with the help of other graceless souls, that you will soon be better; you will repent when the time is better suited to it, and your present situation is changed?

(iii) Or do not some of you labour to put all thoughts of these things far away from you? 'While we are alive, let us live. All will be well with us, though we add drunkenness to thirst.' Isn't it one, or all, of these rotten, corrupt principles that lie at the bottom of your careless walking with God? Beware, I implore you, lest the Lord tear you in pieces!

Sermon 5

Walking Humbly with God (*cont.*)

And to walk humbly with your God.—Mic. 6:8

HAVING told you what is necessary before we can walk with God, we now proceed to the second point.

2. *What walking with God involves*

The expression itself occurs frequently in the Scriptures with many verses referring both to examples of those who did so and to precepts for others to imitate them.

It is said of Enoch that he 'walked with God' (Gen. 5:24). Similarly, 'Noah walked with God' (Gen. 6:9) and Hezekiah 'walked before him' (Isa. 38:3). Abraham is commanded to walk with God (Gen. 17:1), and the same expression, with some little variations, appears almost a hundred times in the Scriptures. Sometimes we are said to 'walk with God'; sometimes to 'walk before him'; sometimes to 'walk after him,' to 'follow hard after him'; sometimes to 'walk in his ways'; all to the same purpose.

The expression, as you know, is metaphorical; by taking an illustration from the natural world, spiritual truths are expressed.

While not pressing the metaphor beyond its main purpose, nor insisting that all its details are to be applied, nor requiring either that it must provide a proof of all that it suggests, what it teaches is that walking with God consists, in general, with the performing of that obedience, in matter and manner, which God in the covenant of grace requires at our hands.

I will note a few of the chief elements of this obedience, brought to life and significance by the metaphor:

(i) *In order that our obedience should be a true walking with God, it is necessary that we should be in covenant with him, and that the obedience offered is according to the nature of that covenant.*

This was mentioned previously when discussing what is required to walk with God, namely, that we should have peace and agreement with him. Here it is formally considered, as it arises in the phrase 'with God': the spring and rule of our obedience. This expression comprehends all of that duty which pertains to us in the covenant. As the words 'I am God Almighty' or 'All-sufficient' (Gen. 17:1) – that is, 'To you, I will be so' – comprehend the whole of the covenant on God's part, that he will be for us an all-sufficient God, so the words that follow contain the whole of our duty: 'Walk before me.' Their meaning is explained by the phrase that follows: 'and be blameless.' The covenant, the agreement that exists between God and us in Christ, in which he promises to be our God, and we give ourselves up to be his people, is the spring and foundation of that obedience which defines walking with God. It involves being in an agreement with him, in covenant with him. Outside of that covenant, we can have no dealings whatsoever.

(ii) *It is an obedience that accords with the nature and character of that covenant* in which we are agreed with God. Walking with God according to the tenor of the law of works was, 'Do this and live.' The situation is now changed. The rule now is that of Genesis 17:1, '"Walk before me and be blameless," or upright, in all the obedience that I require of you.'

There are various requirements for walking with God in obedience if it is to answer the character of the covenant in which we are agreed:

(a) It must proceed from faith in God, by Christ the mediator. Faith in God in general is, and must be, the principle of all obedience in any covenant (Heb. 11:6), but faith in God through Christ the mediator is the only acceptable principle of that obedience which accords with the tenor of the new covenant. This is why it is called 'the obedience of faith' (Rom. 1:5), that is, of faith in God by Christ (as the context demands). His blood is the blood of this covenant (Heb. 9:15, 10:29). The covenant itself is confirmed and ratified by it, and by the blood of that covenant we receive everything that is to be received from God (Zech. 9:11). Whenever God, therefore, mentions the covenant to Abraham, and stirs him up to the obedience required in it, he continually mentions 'the seed, the offspring'; 'who,' says the apostle, 'is Christ' (Gal. 3:16). As it is said, in general, that 'whoever would draw near to God must believe that he exists,' so, in particular, with respect to the new covenant, Christ says of himself, 'I am the way.' There is no going to the Father but by him (John 14:6). Those who have believed in God must 'be careful to devote themselves to good works' (Titus 3:8);

that is, those who have believed in God through Christ. If in our obedience we walk with God according to the tenor of the new covenant, that obedience is the fruit of justifying faith; it is faith in God through Christ.

(b) It is an obedience that must be perfect; that is, the person must be perfect, or upright, in his or her walk. 'Walk before me and be blameless' (Gen. 17:1). It was said of Noah that he was 'blameless in his generation' (Gen. 6:9), and many others are described in the same way. David tells us to 'mark the blameless' (Psa. 37:37); that is, those who walk according to the character of the new covenant. And our Saviour, calling for this obedience, commands us to 'be perfect, as your heavenly Father is perfect' (Matt. 5:48).

Now, there is a twofold perfection:

1. There is a complete righteousness. With this sense, the law is described as making 'nothing perfect' (Heb. 7:19); bringing nothing to a complete righteousness. And the sacrifices cannot 'make perfect those who draw near' (Heb. 10:1). They could not consummate the work of righteousness being aimed at. With this sense, also, we are said to be perfect, 'complete,' in Christ (Col. 2:10 KJV), and our beauty is said to be 'perfect' (Ezek. 16:14) through Christ's comeliness. This is the perfection of justification, which we are not presently considering.

2. But there is a perfection within us. This also is twofold: there is a complete perfection of joy, and there is a perfect tendency towards that joy.

1. With respect to the first, Paul tells us that he was not yet made perfect (Phil. 3:12). But we are told where and by whom this is to be obtained: 'the spirits of the righteous

made perfect' (Heb. 12:23). The righteous are not made perfect in this way until they are brought into the presence of God. This perfection is the goal of Christ's redemption (Eph. 5:25, 26) and of all their obedience (Eph. 4:13, 14). But this is not the perfection required by the covenant, but that to which it brings us, as, according to its promise, we are carried on in the work of 'bringing holiness to completion in the fear of God' (2 Cor. 7:1; see also Job 9:20).

2. There is also the perfection involved as we tend to this goal. Noah and Job are said to be perfect, and Abraham is commanded to be perfect; David, also, describes the happiness of the perfect man. In this respect, notice:

(i) There is no discussion in Scripture of this perfection where its application is limited to such an absolute perfection that would not admit any degree of failing, or defect. The Hebrew word used with respect to Noah (Gen. 6:9) and in the terms of the covenant relating to Abraham (Gen. 17:1) has different implications. When spoken in the abstract it signifies 'simplicity of manners,' without guile (cf. Rom. 16:18 'simple,' KJV 'naive,' ESV). Describing Jacob in Genesis 25:27 (KJV), the word is rendered 'a plain man,' meaning plainhearted, without guile – just as Christ speaks of Nathanael. This sense of the word is found in the notable example (1 Kings 22:34) where the man who killed Ahab is said to draw his bow 'at random,' that is, without any specific pernicious purpose. In Job 9:20 the word is contrasted with an adjective rendered 'perverse,' that is, 'unquiet, malicious.' In the New Testament, such a man is said to be 'one who cannot justly be blamed' or reproved 'for dealing perversely.' Many other examples might be given. There is a further Hebrew word, often rendered 'upright,' also used for this purpose, but as it is generally accepted that this word in Scripture goes no further than 'integrity,' and does not imply absolute perfection, I need not comment on it.

(ii) Two things are involved in this perfection of obedience required in our walking with God in the new covenant. The first has to do with our obedience, and the second with the persons obeying.

1. The perfection with respect to the obedience itself, our objective obedience, has to do with the parts, or the whole, of the will and counsel of God. The law, or will of God, with respect to our obedience is perfect; it contains its own integrity. And we must have respect to all the parts of it that are revealed to us. We find this in David: 'having my eyes fixed on all your commandments' (Psa. 119:6); see also James 2:10.

2. Subjective perfection, with respect to the person obeying, involves his sincerity and freedom from guile – the uprightness of his heart in his obedience. This is what is mainly intended in the expressions, 'Be blameless,' 'the perfect man' – being upright, without guile, hypocrisy, false or selfish purposes – in singleness and simplicity of heart doing the whole will of God.

This, then, is that perfect obedience which is involved in walking with God. Whatever comes short of this – if the heart is not upright, not free of hypocrisy or selfishness; if the obedience is not universal – it is not walking with God. Its perfection lies in its aim towards completeness. It is that which Paul wished for the Corinthians (2 Cor. 13:9; 'even your perfection,' KJV), and to which he exhorted the

Hebrews (Heb. 6:1, 'go on to maturity'; 'to perfection,' KJV).
If we fail, or come short of this perfection, through any
deceit of heart, by consciously retaining any sweet morsel
under our tongue, by keeping a knee for a Baal or a bow
for Rimmon, we do not walk with God. It is sad to think of
how many lose all that they have done, or have achieved,
by coming short of this perfection. One vile lust or another
– love of the world, pride, ambition, laziness, hard-heart-
edness – may lose everything, spoil all; and men walk contrary to God when they think they are walking with him
most.

(iii) *For our obedience to be a true walk with God it is necessary for it to be a constant, progressive motion towards a fixed
goal.* Walking is a constant progress. If someone is walking
towards some destination, he may perhaps stumble and
even fall; but while his purpose and effort are still directed
towards his goal – while he does not remain where he fell
but gets up again and presses forward – he is still, because
of his determination to proceed, said to be walking in that
way. But if this man sits down, or lies down in the way, you
cannot say that he is walking. Much less can you say it if he
goes off in the opposite direction. It is the same with that
obedience involved in walking with God. 'I press on,' says
the apostle, 'towards the goal' (Phil. 3:14); 'I press on' (Phil.
3:12). 'So run that you may obtain,' he tells us (1 Cor. 9:24).
'My soul followeth hard after thee,' says David (Psa. 63:8,
KJV). The enjoyment of God in Christ is the goal before us;
our walking is a constant pressing towards it. To fall into
temptation, or even fall under it, is no hindrance, as long as
the man may be said to be walking, even though he might

not be making great speed, and though he might have defiled himself by his fall. Not every omission of duty and not every commission of sin disqualifies us from continuing in our duty. But to sit down, or to give up – to continue in the path and course of sin – this is what is called walking contrary to God, and not with him.

(iv) *Walking with God is to walk always as under God's eye.* It is therefore called 'walking before him,' before his face, in his sight. To walk with him means that all the duties of obedience are performed under the eye of God.

There are two ways by which a man may do all things as under God's eye:

(a) By a general apprehension of God's omniscience and presence, in that 'all are naked and exposed to the eyes of him' (Heb. 4:13). This is that realisation that he knows all things; that his understanding is infinite; that nothing can be hidden from him; that there is no escaping his presence (Psa. 139:7), no hiding from him, the darkness is light to him. Men may have a general persuasion that they are under God's eye, and all are conscious of this. I don't say that all are actually persuaded of it, but the innate sense of it within them will, if allowed to act freely, make them know it and consider it (Psa. 94:9; Job 24:23; Prov. 15:3).

(b) By a performing of obedience under God's eye, with a sense that God is deeply concerned with our obedience. God told David, '"I will counsel you with my eye upon you" (Psa. 32:8). The consideration of my eye being upon you will instruct you and teach you in the way in which you should go. My eye is on you as one who is concerned in your ways and obedience.' This is walking with God: considering him as looking on us, deeply concerned in all our ways, walk and obedience.

We may view the Lord, in this concern he has for us, as one from whom we receive:

1. direction;
2. protection;
3. examination and trial.

1. *Direction*: 'I will counsel you with my eye upon you.' A sense of God's eye upon us sends us to him for guidance and direction in the whole course of our obedience. If a child is walking with his father's eye upon him, then, if at any point he becomes uncertain of the direction he should go, will he not ask his father, who knows the way and sees exactly where he is? Are we at any loss in our way? Do we not know what to do, or how to steer our course? Let us look to him whose eye is upon us and we shall be directed (Prov. 22:12).

2. *Protection*: His eyes are upon us, and his ears open to us, so as to give us protection and deliverance (Psa. 34:15), and to give it fully (2 Chron. 16:9). This is one reason why the eyes of God are upon his people and their ways: that he may 'give strong support' to them. 'I have seen it' lies behind all their deliverances.

3. *Examination and trial*: His eyes are upon us 'to test the children of man' (Psa. 11:4, 5); to search and to try, as David says, 'and see if there be any grievous way' in us. This is the application he makes, following his consideration of God's omnipresence and omniscience (Psa. 139:7-18). Having presented God's intimate knowledge of, and acquaintance

with him and all his ways, he makes use of it by appealing to God with respect to his integrity in his obedience (verses 23, 24). Job speaks to God in the same way, 'Have you eyes of flesh? Do you see as man sees?' (Job 10:4); that is, 'You do not.' And to what does this refer? To God's testing the paths and obedience of the sons of men (Job 10:6). When our Saviour comes to try, examine and search the obedience of his churches, he is said to have eyes 'like a flame of fire' (Rev. 1:14). And while doing so, he tells his churches, 'I know your works,' or 'I have not found you perfect; I have something against you'; all of which is evidence of his trial and examination of their obedience.

This is what walking before God, or under his eye, means: it is to consider him looking at us specifically, as someone concerned with our ways, our walk and our obedience. It is to take counsel from him continually, to fly to him for protection, to consider that he weighs and tries all our ways and works, to see whether they are perfect according to the character of the covenant of grace.

There are two things that will most certainly follow from such a consideration of our walk with God, under his eye and control:

1. There will be *reverential thoughts of him*. This God, who is a consuming fire, is near to us; his eyes are always on us. 'Let us be grateful,' says the apostle, 'and … let us offer to God acceptable worship with reverence and awe' (Heb. 12:28, 29). If men are careful about their behaviour and bearing, at the very least, in order to appear reverent before their rulers and governors who only see the outside, should we not regard Him who has his eye always upon us,

who searches our hearts and tries our reins, the innermost secrets of our soul?

2. *Self-abasement*, under a sense of our great vileness and of the imperfection of all our works. But both these points belong properly to our next consideration: what it means to walk humbly before God.

(v) *Walking with God in our obedience involves a pleasure and delight in the walk; in it we are bound to God in his ways and with the cords of love.* Anyone who travels with another unwillingly, by compulsion, with every step being a weariness and a burden to him, and whose whole heart longs to be released from his company, can hardly be said to be walking with him (at least, no further than mere mechanical motion together). The Lord walks with us and he rejoices over us and in us (Zeph. 3:17); he expresses his delight in the various services we offer him (Song of Sol. 2:14). The Son and Wisdom of God tells us the same (Prov. 8:31); his joy and delight is in the obedience of the children of man. This is why we have those longing expressions of God for the obedience of his people, '"Oh that they had such a mind as this always, to fear me" (Deut. 5:29). Turn, turn; when will you turn? What have you seen in me, that you have gone away?' And our Saviour, the husband of the church, raises this to the greatest height imaginable (Song of Sol. 4:9-16). He speaks as if transported by a delight that is almost unbearable, which he receives from the love and obedience of his spouse, comparing it to things of the highest natural delight and preferring it far more.

Now, surely, if God has this delight in us as we walk before him, is it not to be expected that we should delight in him in our obedience? It is not my present business to repeat the testimonies of Scripture in which we are either required to delight in the Lord, or to note the example of saints who have done so, nor to insist on the nature of that delight. Job states that the sure mark of a hypocrite is that, notwithstanding all his obedience, 'Will he take delight in the Almighty?' (Job 27:10). But note this at least, there is a twofold character to this delight:

1. A delight in the obedience itself, and in its duties;
2. A delight in God in that obedience.

1. There may be a delight in other aspects of the duty of obedience even when there is no delight in God in it. A man may delight to accompany another in the way because of some pleasantness in the journey, or for any other reasons which may attract him, though he may have no delight at all in the fellowship of his companion. God tells us of hypocritical people who seek him daily, who are delighted to know his ways and to approach him (Isa. 58:2). It is said of some that Ezekiel's voice was to them as 'a very lovely song of one that hath a pleasant voice' (Ezek. 33:31, 32, KJV). There may be something in the ministry of the ordinations of God; in the person ministering; in the things ministered, which attract the minds of hypocrites so that they run after them and attend them with much voracious delight. John was 'a burning and shining lamp,' said the Saviour to the wicked Jews, and 'you were willing to rejoice for a while in his light' (John 5:35). How many have we seen, running after sermons, pressing with the multitude, finding sweetness and contentment in the word, who yet have nothing but novelty, or the ability of

the preacher, or some other outward consideration, as the cause of their delight.

2. There is a delight in God in our obedience. 'Delight yourself in the Lord,' says the Psalmist (Psa. 37:4), and a delight in obedience and duties because these are his will and his ways. When a person aims to meet with God in every duty, and to have fellowship with him, to communicate his soul to him, and to receive refreshment from him; when on this account our duties and all our ways of obedience are sweet and pleasant to us: then we certainly walk with God in them.

Application

1. *For our direction.* Understand that it is a great thing to walk with God as we ought. We have previously heard how many things are required for it to be acceptable, and now we have considered some of the things of which it consists. Who has prepared his heart to walk with God as he ought? Who believes that his walk is what it should be? Believe me, friends, a formal performance of duties out of habit, from one day and one week to another, both in private and in public, comes very short of this walking with God. Men are contented with very slight and formal efforts. They pray, morning and evening; they take part with some of the people of God against open profane men; they keep themselves from those sins that would wound a natural conscience – all is well with them. But do not be deceived. To walk with God requires:

(i) All the strength and vigour of the soul. 'You shall love the Lord your God with all your heart.' The soul and heart of a man is to be in this work; he must plan and organize for it; he must fight for it. Formality and habit will not do.

(ii) That the new covenant in its universality must be complete in it, in all sincerity. It involves not merely doing this thing or that thing, but doing all things commanded by Christ: not loving friends only, but enemies also; not denying the ways of ungodly men only, but denying self and the world; not merely hurting no one, but doing good to all; not hating only the actions of evil men, but loving their persons; not praying and hearing only, but giving alms, being friendly, showing mercy, exercising loving-kindness in the earth; not a mortification of pride and vanity only, especially in the outward expression of them to others, but mortification of envy, anger and discontent also. In a word, what is required is 'bringing holiness to completion in the fear of God' (2 Cor. 7:1). If men who profess religion but are almost eaten up by the world or the flesh, by envy, party-spirit, laziness or uselessness in their generation, were to open their hearts to the rules we have been discussing, they would find that they have very little reason to be satisfied with their ways and walking.

2. *For the direction of others*. In the light of all the truths that have been mentioned, I would only ask one thing: Do you wish to be known as one who walks with God?

(i) What evidence do you have that you are in covenant with him; that your covenant with hell and death is broken, and that you are taken into the bond of the covenant of grace? What account can you give to God, to others, or to your own soul, of your covenant state and condition? How many are at a loss with respect to this, the foundation of all walking with God!

(ii) Does your obedience stem from faith? What evidence do you have for this? Go over all the causes, effects and adjuncts of a justifying faith, and test whether you have this principle of all acceptable obedience. How has it been wrought in you? What work of the Spirit have you had upon you? What has been your conviction, your humiliations, your conversion? When, how, by what means did they ensue? Are your hearts purified by them, and are you baptized into one Spirit with the people of God? Or are you still enemies to them?

(iii) Is your walking universal and complete, according to the tenor of the covenant? Do you keep a sweet morsel under your tongue, a beloved lust that is indulged, a reserved sin, which you still cannot thoroughly part with?

(iv) Do you delight in God in the obedience you yield to him? Or are his ways a burden to you, which you are scarcely able to bear: weary of private prayer, of Sundays, of all the worship of God? I leave these matters to your conscience.

Sermon 6

Walking Humbly with God (*cont.*)

And to walk humbly with your God.—Mic. 6:8

I HAVE described what walking with God involves; we next have to consider:

II. *What is the further duty required by the addition of the qualification 'humbly'?*

Of the many important qualifications defining the obedience of believers, that which stands in the foreground and has priority is the following: To 'humble yourself as you walk,' or, to 'walk with God.'

One might conclude that it is such an honour and advancement for a poor sinful creature to be accepted into God's company and to walk with him that he might need to prepare himself for it beforehand by thinking more of himself. 'Is it a small thing,' asks David, 'to be the son-in-law of the king?' 'Is it a small thing to walk with God? The heart of a man who has such a prospect before him should be proud!' But the truth of the matter is completely the opposite. Anyone who wishes to have his heart lifted up to God must make sure that he keeps it down in himself.

There is a natural pride in every man's heart, lifting him up and swelling him, until he is too high and big for God to walk with him.

There are two remarkable things about our walking with God: firstly, the inward power of it; secondly, the outward privilege of it, in regard to the access it provides to its duties. The first builds us up in these duties; the latter only puffs up. These Jews here and their successors, the Pharisees, having received the privilege of walking with God, were, like Capernaum, lifted up into heaven. Trusting in themselves that they were righteous, they despised others; of all men, therefore, they were the most abhorred by God. This is what the Holy Spirit fights against most of all: a resting in the privilege of access. God tells us of the Prince of Tyre that he made his heart 'like the heart of a god' (Ezek. 28:6). He wished to be on equal terms with God, independent, the author of his own good, fearless. This, to some degree, is the state of the heart of every man by nature; a condition which, in fact, is not to be compared to God, but to the devil.

To prevent this evil, I will consider what is being required of us here under two headings:

1. To what are we to submit when humbling ourselves to walk with God?

2. How are we to do this?

1. *There are two things to which we are to submit ourselves in our walk with God*: 1. *The law of his grace*; 2. *The law of his providence*.

(a) In all our walk with God we are to humble ourselves by submitting to the law and rule of his grace. This is the way that he has revealed to us in which he will walk with sinners. The apostle tells us often of the Jews who had wished to walk with God: they had 'a zeal for God.' This is how he himself had been in his days as a Pharisee (Phil. 3:6). He was 'zealous for God' (Acts 22:3), and so were the Jews: 'I bear them witness that they have a zeal for God' (Rom. 10:2). And they pursued righteousness, the 'law that would lead to righteousness' (Rom. 9:31). They took pains 'to establish' their righteousness (Rom. 10:3). What more could be required in order to walk with God than a zeal for him, for his laws and ways, and for a diligent effort to maintain a righteousness before him? How few there are who achieve this much! What reputation such people gain in the world! Yet, says the apostle, they do not succeed in walking with God nor in obtaining that righteousness. Why was that? Because in their attempt to walk with God they did not submit to the law of his grace. They went about seeking to establish their own righteousness and did not submit to the righteousness of God. What righteousness is that? It is the righteousness of faith, according to the law of grace (Rom. 1:17). 'They did not pursue it by faith but as if it were based on works' (Rom. 9:32). The foundation for all this is described in the next verse. We find there two different effects of Christ on different people. Some stumble over him and so are not able to walk on with God. Who are these? Paul tells us in verse 33. Others are not ashamed. Who are they? Those who believe, and so submit to the law of God's grace. Clearly then, men may labour to walk with God and yet still stumble and fall, because they fail to humble themselves before the law of his grace.

Let us see then how this may be done, and what it requires:

1. The basis of the whole of a man's obedience must be this: that in himself he is a lost, hopeless creature, an object of wrath, and that *whatever he may obtain of God must be obtained by way of mere mercy and grace.* It is to this apprehension of himself that proud man (who longs to feel that he has something of his own) must submit to. God abhors everyone who approaches him while trusting in any other basis. Our Saviour Christ has revealed to men what they are, and what they must be, if they will come to God by him. 'I came,' he said, 'to save that which is lost' (Matt. 18:11, KJV). 'I came, not to call the righteous, but sinners' (Matt. 9:13). 'Those who are well have no need of a physician, but those who are sick' (Matt. 9:12). 'I came into this world,' he said, 'that those who do not see may see, and those who see may become blind' (John 9:39). In summary, he said, 'If you intend to have anything to do with God through me, you must see yourselves as lost sinners: blind, sick, dead. So that whatever you obtain, must be obtained by way of grace alone.'

How was this instruction followed by Paul? Do you wish to understand the basis of his obedience? We are shown it in 1 Timothy 1:13-15. 'I was like this and like that; I am the foremost of sinners; "but I received mercy." It is only on account of mercy and grace that I have anything from God.' This principle he emphasises further in Philippians 3:7-9, 'All is lost; all is rubbish; Christ is all in all.' The proud Pharisees could not submit to this. It is the main issue in many of their disputes with the Saviour. To be lost, blind, nothing – they could not endure hearing this. Were they not the children of Abraham? Did they not do such and such? To be told that they were lost and nothing, could only be the result of envy. And on this rock, thousands dash themselves in our days. When they are convicted that there is a need to walk with God (as, at one time or another and by one means or another, most men are), they then set out to fulfil those duties which they have neglected, and that obedience which they think is acceptable, continuing in this course while that conviction remains. But they do not humble themselves to fulfil this part of the law of God's grace – to be vile, miserable, lost, cursed, hopeless in themselves. They never make a thorough work of this. They lay the founda- tion of their obedience in mud, which should first have been dug out, and they stumble at the stumbling-stone in their very first attempt to walk with God.

There are two evils involved in the mere performance of this duty of being humbled which utterly frustrate all the attempts of such men to walk with God:

(i) The first is that men, without humility, will set out, to some extent at least, to walk with God in their own strength. 'Why can we do nothing?' ask the Pharisees. 'Are we also blind?' Acting in one's own power is natural to such people and cannot be separated from them. It steals upon them in every duty they attempt to perform. But nothing is more completely opposite to the whole nature of gospel obedience than this, that a man should fulfil the least of it in his own strength, without the real influence of life and power from God in Christ. 'Apart from me,' says Christ, 'you can do nothing' (John 15:5). All that is achieved without strength from him is nothing. God works in us 'both to will and to work for his good pleasure' (Phil. 2:13). Whatever a man does, which is not worked in him by God, for which he does not receive strength from Christ, is all lost, all perishing. And our obtaining of strength from Christ for every duty is based on that submission to the law of grace which we are considering.

(ii) Secondly, this obedience, without humility, will strengthen men in their present condition, directing them towards hell and destruction. I will speak more of this later.

2. We are next to humble ourselves before the law of grace by a firm conviction, exerting itself effectively in all our obedience, that no righteousness can be obtained before God by any of our performances of duty and obedience whatsoever. The apostle goes to some lengths to show that this is part of the law of God's grace. 'If,' he says, 'righteousness comes by the law' (that is, by our obedience to God according to the law) 'then faith and the promise are null and void' (Rom. 4:13-15). There is an inconsistency between the law of grace (that is, of faith and promise) and the obtaining of righteousness before God by obedience. 'If justification were through the law, then Christ died for no purpose' (Gal. 2:21). 'You wish to walk with God according to his mind? You wish to please him in Jesus Christ? What do you do? You strive to perform the duties required of you in order that, *on their account*, you might be accepted righteous by God.' 'I tell you,' says the apostle, 'if this is how things are, "Christ died for no purpose." If this is a righteousness before God, obtained by things that you can do, the gospel is to no purpose.'

To this, also, the proud heart of man must humble itself if he is to walk with God: he must obey, he must fulfil duties, he must be holy, he must abstain from every sin. But he must do all this under a living, active conviction that by these things a righteousness before God is not to be obtained. This must influence all your duties, guide you in your whole course of obedience, and accompany you in its every act. How few are influenced by this conviction in their walk with God! Don't most men proceed on different practical principles? Don't they build up confidence for their appearance before God from their own stock of obedience?

3. In the midst of all our obedience, which is our own, we must believe and accept a righteousness which is not our own, nor in any way wrought or obtained by us. We have no assurance that any such righteousness exists but by the faith we have in the promise of God, and on that promise, renouncing all that is in or of ourselves, we must merely, and solely, rest for our righteousness and acceptance with him.

This is that humility which Paul testifies is found in his own heart, as mentioned before (Phil. 3:7-9). He reckons up all his own duties – surrounded by them, he sees them lying around him on all sides; each one of them offering its assistance, making itself look beautiful, and crying that it is 'gain' – 'But,' says the apostle, 'you are all loss and rubbish.' I look for another righteousness, one that's very different from anything that you can give me.

Man sees and knows his own righteousness and walk with God. He sees what it costs him, and where it places him. He knows what pains he has taken to obtain it; what waiting, fasting, labouring and praying it has cost him. He knows how he has deprived himself of his natural desires and mortified his flesh in abstaining from sin. These are the things of a man, wrought in him, performed by him; and the spirit of a man knows them. These provide a fair promise to the man who has been sincere in them, for whatever goal or purpose he would use them. But as for the righteousness of Christ, that is outside of himself, he does not see it, nor has he experienced it. The spirit which is within him knows nothing of it. He has no acquaintance with it except as it is revealed and offered in the promises. And these, even, do not tell him that this righteousness is his – provided for him in particular – but only that it is promised to and provided for believers. Now, for a man to throw away that which he can see in order to obtain what he cannot see – to refuse that which promises to supply him with some support and good hope in God's presence, and which he knows belongs to him and cannot be taken away from him; to throw it away for something which he must take by faith, based upon the word of a promise, and in spite of ten thousand doubts, fears and temptations that it does not in fact belong to him – such a step requires the soul to be humbled before God, something which a man's heart is not easily brought to.

Every man must hazard his future state and condition. The question is, upon what will he place his trust? Our own obedience is at hand and offers a fair promise of assistance and help. For a man therefore to throw this aside completely and trust to the naked promise of God to receive him in Jesus Christ, is something for which the heart of man must be humbled before he can bring himself to do it. Everything in the man will protest against this captivity of itself. Innumerable proud arguments and thoughts will present themselves against it. And even when the rational mind and soul is convicted by the truth, the practical principles of the will and affections will fight fiercely against it. But this is the law of God's grace, which must be submitted to, if we are to walk with him. The most holy, wise and zealous, who have yielded their constant obedience to God, whose good works and godly conversation have shone as lights in the world, must cast down all these crowns at the foot of Jesus. They must renounce all for him and for the righteousness which he has wrought for us. All must be sold for the pearl. All must be parted with for Christ. While following the strictest course of obedience in us, we are still to look for a righteousness which is completely from outside us.

4. We must humble ourselves to establish our obedience on a completely new basis but continue to pursue it with just as much diligence as if it still stood upon the old basis. 'For by grace you have been saved through faith. And this is not your own doing; it is the gift of God, not a result of works, so that no one may boast. For we are his workmanship, created in Christ Jesus for good works, which God prepared beforehand that we should walk in them' (Eph. 2:8-10).

'But if not as a result of works, why is there now any need of good works at all? Our obedience was required at the first so that we might be saved. But this requirement, it seems, has now been taken away: our works and duties are excluded from contributing in any way towards our salvation. For if it is by works, then "grace would no longer be grace" (Rom. 11:6). Let us, therefore, put aside all works and obedience, so that grace may abound.'

It is clear that this is how many did, and others still do, make use of this grace of God: turning it into permissiveness.

'But there is more to be said about good works than this,' says the apostle. 'Their legal goal is changed and the old foundation upon which they stood has been taken away. But there is a new constitution that makes them necessary; a new obligation, which requires that we fulfil them just as carefully as we did formerly.' We find it in the first reference above, 'We are his workmanship, created in Christ Jesus for good works' (Eph. 2:10). Having saved us by grace, God has, on that account, appointed us to walk in obedience. Here is the difference: 'before, I was to perform good works because I was to be saved by them. I must perform them now because I am saved without them.' God, saving us in Christ by grace, has appointed that we should now perform those works, which previously we did in order to be saved, as a way of acknowledging our free salvation. Though works left no room at all for grace, yet grace leaves room for works, though not such room as they had before grace came. This, then, is that to which we have to humble ourselves: to be as diligent in good works and obedient duties, because we are saved without them, as we would be if we could be saved by them. A man who walks with God must humble his soul to place all his obedience on this footing. He has saved us freely; now let our manner of life be worthy of the gospel.

Paul shows how this principle is effective in believers to the crucifying of all sins. 'Sin will have no dominion over you,' he says, 'since you are not under law but under grace' (Rom. 6:14). Worldly reason would argue very differently. 'If we are not under law,' it would say, 'that is, the condemning power of the law, then let sin have its dominion, power and rule. Wasn't it the law that forbade sin, under pain of damnation: "Cursed be everyone who does not abide …, etc."? Didn't the law command obedience, with the promise of salvation: "The one who does them shall live by them" (Gal. 3:10-12)? If then the law has no more power over us, in forbidding sin with its terror of damnation, or commanding obedience if we wish for righteousness and salvation, why do we need to fulfil the one or avoid the other?' 'Why?' answers the apostle. 'Well, for this reason: that "we are under grace"; which, with its new purposes, and based on new motives and considerations, requires obedience and forbids sin.'

Do we constantly submit ourselves to this part of the law of God's grace – building up and establishing our obedience on grace, and not on the law? motivated by love, and not fear? from what God has done for us in Christ, rather than from what we expect in the future – because 'the free gift of God is eternal life in Christ Jesus our Lord'?

5. Again, we are to humble ourselves to this: that we have to address ourselves to perform the greatest duties, knowing full well that we do not have the strength for the least duty. This is what is so contrary to flesh and blood that our souls must be humbled before we can ever be brought to it. Yet, without this, there is no walking with God. There are great and mighty deeds to be performed in our walk with God in gospel obedience: there is the cutting off of right hands; the plucking out of right eyes; the denying – even the hating, relatively speaking – of fathers, mothers and all relations; dying for Christ; laying down our lives for the brethren; crucifying the flesh; cutting short all earthly desires; keeping the body under subjection; bearing the cross; self-denial, and so on. When these are put into

practice, we will find them to be great and mighty deeds. This is what is required in the law of grace: that we undertake to carry these out throughout our days, with a certain knowledge and persuasion that we do not have the strength of ourselves to perform the least of them. We are not 'sufficient in ourselves,' says the apostle (2 Cor. 3:5). We cannot think a good thought. Without Christ we can do nothing (John 15:5). To a carnal heart, this looks like making bricks without straw. 'This is a hard saying. Who can listen to it?' It is to be expected that men should sit down and say, 'Why does he still find fault? Is he not a hard man, reaping where he did not sow? Are his ways right?' Yes, indeed, most right, just and gracious; because his purpose in dealing with us in this way is that when we approach any duty we should look to him, from whom come all our supplies, and in doing so receive strength for what we have to do. How unable was Peter to walk on water! Yet, when Christ called him to come, he ventured into the midst of the sea, and with the command, strength was communicated to support him. God may call us to do or suffer what he pleases, in that his call has an accompanying efficacy that communicates strength to fulfil what he calls us to do (Phil. 1:29).

We are to submit ourselves – not only to conclude, in general, that the duties required of us are not proportional to the strength that resides in us but to the supply laid up for us in Christ – but also to believe that this is the case for every particular duty which we take on. This would be the greatest madness in the world in all natural, worldly matters. You could not discourage a man more than by telling him that he does not have the strength or ability to perform a task that he might be attempting. Once he is convinced of that, it would be the end of all his endeavours, for who would wear himself out over something which is impossible to achieve? But it is different in spiritual matters. God may require from us anything for which there is strength laid up in Christ, enough strength to enable us to fulfil it. And we may, by faith, attempt any duty, however great it may be, if there is grace to be obtained for it from Christ. This is the explanation for those great things done by believers by faith – utterly beyond their own strength and power – those who 'were made strong out of weakness' (Heb. 11:33, 34). When they entered upon the duty, they were weakness itself, but as they attempted it, they grew strong by the supply that was administered to them. In this way we are said to come to Christ 'to find grace to help in time of need' (Heb. 4:16); those times when we are engaged upon a work for which we have no might or power.

This is the way to walk with God: to be ready and willing to undergo any duty, though it might be so much above or beyond our strength, in our belief that there is a supply in Christ. The truth is that anyone who considers what God requires of believers might conclude that they possessed a stock of spiritual strength equal to Samson's, in that they have to fight with principalities and powers, to contend with the world, the self, and so much more. But as he observes them he will quickly notice their weakness and inability. This is where the mystery of it all lies: the duties required of them are in proportion to the grace laid up for them in Christ, not to any strength entrusted to themselves at any time.

6. Another thing to which we must submit ourselves is to be content to have the sharpest afflictions accompanying

our strictest obedience. Men who walk closely with God in this world may, perhaps, have some private assumptions that they will escape trouble in this life, and so they are surprised when a fiery trial comes upon them (1 Pet. 4:12). They become troubled and perplexed and do not know what it means, especially if they see others, who do not know God, prospering and at ease in their lives. Their estates may become ruined, their reputation destroyed, their bodies afflicted with serious diseases, their children being taken away or turning to wickedness and rebellion, their lives in danger every hour, perhaps being killed all the day long. So that they are ready to cry out, with Hezekiah, 'Please, O Lord, remember' (Isa. 38:3), or to dispute the matter, as Job did, when he was in anguish on being disappointed in his hope of dying in his nest. But this attitude is completely opposed to the law of the grace of God, which requires that the children he receives are to be chastised (Heb. 12:6); that they are to endure whatever chastening he calls them to; for, having made the founder of their salvation perfect through all kinds of suffering, he will make his children conformable to him. This, I say, is part of the law of God's grace, that in our highest point of obedience we willingly endure the greatest afflictions. The process of this truth in the relationship between Job and God is worthy of careful study, for although Job argued long with God, yet God did not leave him until he had brought him to acknowledge this truth, and to submit to it with all his heart. This point will arise again under my second heading of submitting to the law of the providence of God. The truth is that to help our poor weak hearts in this matter, to prevent all sinful complaining, arguing, etc., God has established such a provision of safeguards that will enable us to receive it sweetly and with ease. Thus:

(i) He does not correct us for his pleasure, but in order to make us partakers of his holiness, so that we will never be in heaviness unless it is necessary for us. We can rest in this, even if we cannot see the reason or understand the circumstances of our visitation. But because of this truth, we may rest on his sovereign will and wisdom.

(ii) He will work all things together for our good. This takes the poison out of every cup that we drink; indeed, all the bitterness of it. We have concerns which lie far above everything that we suffer or undergo here, and if all works for our advantage and improvement, why should it not be welcome to us?

(iii) It is in this way that conformity and likeness to Jesus Christ is to be attained here on earth.

Various other principles arise which prevail upon our hearts to humble and submit our souls to this part of the law of God's grace. The devil never thought that Job could be brought to this, and he was therefore restless until he was allowed to put him to the test. But he was disappointed and conquered, and his condemnation was all the greater.

This then is the first thing required of us if we are to walk humbly before God: we are to submit to the law of God's grace. Let us conclude by observing some applications of this.

Application 1

Let us examine ourselves to see if this is true of us. We fulfil our duties and so seem to be walking with God, but:

(i) Is our obedience based on a deep apprehension and a full conviction of our own vileness and nothingness – of our being the chief of sinners, lost and undone – so that we always lie at the foot of sovereign grace and mercy? Is this truly so? In which case, when, how, and by what means was this conviction brought upon us? I do not mean a mere sense of being a sinner, but a specific conviction of our lost, undone condition, producing appropriate feelings within us. Do we cry to the Lord out of the depths? Or is the purpose of our obedience an endeavour to avoid falling into such a state? I am afraid that many amongst us (if it were possible for us to dive into the depths of our hearts) would be found to be obeying God purely in order to avoid that condition to which we must be brought before we will yield acceptable obedience to him. If we truly intend to walk with God let us be clear about this, that its foundation lies in that sense and apprehension of ourselves that cries out, 'Of sinners, I am chief.'

(ii) Does this always remain in our thoughts and upon our spirits, namely, that by all we have done, all we do, or can do, we will never obtain righteousness to stand in the presence of God? In the secret depths of our hearts, do we judge that none of our righteousness is obtained on this basis? Can we be content to view all our obedience as worthless with respect to obtaining righteousness? Do we appear before God depending simply on another basis, as if there were no such thing as our own obedience in the world? This, indeed, is where the great mystery of gospel obedience lies: that we pursue it with all our strength and might, with all the vigour of our souls, and labour hard to abound in it, as the angels do in their obedience, perfecting holiness in the fear of the Lord. Yet, with respect to the acceptance of our persons, we have no more regard for it than if we had yielded as little obedience as the thief on the cross.

(iii) Are we then humbling ourselves so as to accept the righteousness that God has provided for us in Christ? There is often an active response in the hearts of those whom God is drawing to himself: they do not dare believe the promise; they hardly dare to accept Christ and his righteousness; it would be presumption in them. In most cases this is indeed true of them: such a response does not arise from fear or humility, but *pride*. Men do not know how to humble themselves to receive, on the basis of God's testimony, a righteousness which is completely outside of themselves. The heart is not willing for it. What we are willing to do is to establish our own righteousness and not submit to God's righteousness.

What is the state of your own souls, therefore? Are we clear on this great point or not? If we are not, then, at best, we are only shuffling with God; we are not walking with him. He does not admit anyone into his presence except those who take the righteousness that he has provided. His soul loathes those who would offer up to him anything in its place; those who are engaged in setting up their own wisdom and righteousness against his.

Application 2

I will conclude with a final application: that if all these things are required from those who would walk with God, what will be the experience, what will become, of those who give no thought to such things? We see some clearly walking in an opposite direction, having no regard for God, or any thought of their final end. Others experience some attacks of conscience, to which they respond by believing that they can heal these feelings of guilt and the sins that cause them, by an easy cry of 'God forgive me.' Some go a little further and are careful in fulfilling spiritual duties, but they are not seeking God in an appropriate way, and he will take issue with them.

Sermon 7

Walking Humbly with God (*cont.*)

And to walk humbly with your God.—Mic. 6:8

You have heard what it means to humble ourselves to the law of God's grace.

(a) I will now explain what is involved in humbling ourselves to the law of his providence.

By the law of his providence, I mean God's sovereign disposal of all the concerns of men by whatever means, order and ways he pleases, according to the rule and infinite reason of his goodness, wisdom, righteousness and truth.

General Observations

1. To explain what humbling ourselves to this law means, *some general observations need to be made:*

(i) There is, and always was, a significant part of God's providential administration of all the things of this world and of all the affairs of men in it, which the highest reason of men could never apprehend and which is contrary to everything within us as mere men: our judgment, affections, or any other property that guides our lives.

'Your judgments,' says David to God, 'are on high, out of his sight' (Psa. 10:5); i.e., out of the sight of man, of whom he is speaking. He is not able to see the basis and reason, the order and beauty of them. 'Your righteousness is like the mountains of God; your judgments are like the great deep' (Psa. 36:6); that is, as the sea, whose depths no one can see, nor can anyone know what is done in its great caverns. There is therefore a height in the judgments of God that can never be measured and a depth that can never be fathomed. Men cannot look into his ways. 'Your way was through the sea, your path through the great waters' (Psa. 77:19). Men must be content to stand on the shore and to admire the works of God, but they can never search out their beauty and excellence. This is Zophar's theme in Job 11:7-12. He speaks of the excellence and perfection of God's works of providence and ends with the following summary of its inscrutable nature: 'Vain man would know the secrets of God's counsels, the reason of his ways; but, in his efforts after it, he is as an ass, as a wild ass, as the colt of an ass' (verse 12, KJV). Nothing could be spoken of with more contempt, abasing the pride of a poor creature.

We know that the ways of God are all perfect. He is our rock, and his work is perfect. Nothing can be added to them or taken away; they are resplendent and beautiful in their season. Nothing comes from him that does not spring from wonderful counsel, and all his ways will, at length, be found to praise him. But, as Job says, we do not see it; we do not perceive it (Job 9:11). We take no notice of it, for 'who has known the mind of the Lord, or who has been his counsellor?' (Rom. 11:33, 34).

It was not only the heathen, therefore, who were perplexed in their views of the workings of providence (some turned to atheism because of it; most ascribed everything to blind, uncertain chance and fate; only a few tried to give some splendour to something they could not understand) but God's people also disputed with him over the equity of his ways. They brought their arguments against him and contended against his wisdom: 'You say, "The way of the Lord is not just"' (Ezek. 18:25); or, again, 'Yet you say, "The way of the Lord is not just"' (Ezek. 33:20). Not only the common people but the best of God's people in the Old Testament were greatly troubled because they often could not see the beauty and excellence, or understand the reason and order, of God's dispensations. I could show this from the experiences of Job, David, Heman, Jeremiah, Habakkuk and others.

In that this is the general case with respect to God's providential actions – that there is much in them that is not only above us and unsearchable to us but also inconsistent with our reason, judgment and feelings – we surely need to submit our souls to this law of providence, if we intend to walk with him. There is no other way of coming to an agreement with him or of keeping our hearts from complaining.

(ii) There are four things in God's providential disposing of the concerns of men in the world that require that we humble ourselves before him, not being in any way able to contend with him: (a) evident confusion; (b) indescribable variety; (c) sudden alterations; (d) deep distresses.

(a) *Evident confusion.* Like that described in Isaiah 8:22. Anyone who surveys the general state of the world will see nothing but distress, trouble and anguish: 'behold, darkness shall cover the earth, and thick darkness the peoples' (Isa. 60:2). The oppression of tyrants, the suppression of nations, the destruction of men and beasts, fury and desolations, abound both in the past and the present. The best and choicest parts of the earth are inhabited by those who do not know God; those who hate him, who fill and replenish the world with habitations of cruelty, playing with evils, like the leviathan in the sea. In this context, God is said to make 'darkness his covering, his canopy around him, thick clouds dark with water' (Psa. 18:11) and to 'dwell in thick darkness' (2 Chron. 6:1). It is the patience and wisdom of the saints to wait for the issue of this providence and to humble themselves to its law.

(b) *Indescribable variety.* So as not to enter into great detail, consider the situation of saints all over the world, and in two contexts:

(1) Comparing ourselves with one another, what indescribable variety of circumstances do we find! Some are continually persecuted; some are continually at peace. Some are in dungeons and prisons; some in liberty in their own homes. The saints of one nation suffer under great oppression through many ages; those of another land live in quietness. In the same places may be found some who are poor and in great distress, being hard put to find their daily bread throughout their lives, whereas others abound in all things. Some are struck with diseases, going softly and mourning all their days; others are spared, hardly touched by the rod at all (and yet, very often, the advantage of holiness and close walking with God is found among those who

are most afflicted). How also does God deal in grace with
families? With some he takes the whole family into covenant, while a generation of another family, whose parents
are no less holy, he passes over completely. He comes into
a household and takes one, leaving another; he takes a
despised outcast, and leaves a favourite. In one family, also,
some are wise, endowed with great gifts and abilities; others
are weak, liable to contempt and reproach. Who could
conclude, by the eye of reason alone, that all are the children of one Father and that he loves them all alike? If you
were to enter a great house and see some children dressed
in scarlet and having all they needed, whereas others were
cutting wood and drawing water, you would conclude that
they were not all children, but that some were children and
others servants. But if you were to be told that they were
all the children of one father, and that the hewers of wood,
living on the bread and waters of affliction and dressed
in tatters, were as dear to him as the others, and that he
intended to leave them as good an inheritance as the others,
then, if you resolved not to question the wisdom and goodness of the father, you would have to submit to his authority
with a quiet subjection of mind. This is how things are in
God's great family; nothing will quieten our minds other
than humbling ourselves to the law of his providence.

(2) Comparing oneself with unbelievers was the great
temptation of many in the past. The cries of Job, David,
Jeremiah and Habakkuk are so well known that I need not
dwell on them.

It is not necessary for me to find further examples of the
variety of the dispensations of God towards the men of the
world, a variety which the wisest of men cannot reduce to

any rule of righteousness. Solomon describes it in Eccles. 9:11. God disposes mankind according to no pattern of expectation which we can discover. This reality disturbed the mind of Marcus Brutus, that mirror of mankind in its natural condition, causing him to cry out, 'O wretched Virtue!'[1]

(c) *Sudden alterations.* In the case of Job, God takes a man (whom he has blessed with the choicest of blessings, in the course of a life of obedience and close walking with God) who expected to die in peace and to see good all his days, and ruins him in a moment. He blasts his name, so that one who was esteemed as a choice saint cannot now save himself from being viewed generally as a hypocrite; slays his children; takes away his rest, health and everything that he desired. This amazes the soul. It does not know what God is doing, nor why he deals with it in what seems such a bitter way. A man in this condition, or one who may fall into this condition, will find that he will never be able to walk with God in it, without humbling himself to the law of God's providence.

(d) *Great, deep and long-lasting distresses* have the same effects as sudden alterations. I will mention these again later.

These are, generally speaking, some of the aspects of God's providential disposal of men's affairs in this world that are too hard and wonderful for flesh and blood. They

---

[1] Quoting a lost Greek tragedy, 'O wretched Virtue, thou wert but a name, and yet I worshipped thee as real indeed; but now, it seems, thou wert but fortune's slave.'

[142]

seem to be paths that lie in the deep; completely opposed to all the rules for procedure which he has given for us to judge things by. We are to judge things once, whereas he will call all things to a second account.

2. Having made these observations, I will now return to what I first proposed, namely, the duty of humbling ourselves to the law of this providence of God, in so far as it concerns us particularly.

I do not mean merely that men should be content with the dealings of God with the world, but that we should humble our hearts before him with respect to those things which relate to ourselves, even when they may involve one or more of the difficulties mentioned above. Our circumstances are very different in this world, and how they may differ even further before we leave it we do not know. Some are in one condition, some in another. That we should not be envious of one another nor of anyone else in the world, that we should not complain against God nor accuse him of folly – that is what I am aiming at. This is so necessary in these days, when even good men find it hard to bear with their own situations, if it in any way differs from that of others.

Submission to the law of God's providence

The next thing, then, is to consider *how and where we are to submit to the law of God's providence*. There are specific things, in this respect, to which our souls must submit:

(i) *God's sovereignty.* May he not do what he wills with his own? This is so clearly answered in Job that I do not need to go any further to confirm it. Job 33:8-13 provides the summary of Job's complaint that, while innocent and obedient, God had dealt harshly with him and brought him to great distress. What answer does he receive? 'Behold, in this you are not right' (verse 12). It is most unrighteous for any man to make such a complaint. Whether Job did so or not may be argued, but for anyone to do so is certainly unjust. On what ground may such an answer be asserted? Look at the words following: '"God is greater than man. Why do you contend against him?" There is no purpose in arguing with God, who is mightier than you. It is also unjust to argue with One who is so infinitely and incomparably mighty in his absolute dominion and sovereignty. "He will answer none of man's words," "For," he says, "he will give no account of his ways." He disposes all things as he wills and as he pleases.' This answer is developed, reaching a conclusion in Job 34:18, 19. Men will not openly revile and complain against their rulers; what then shall be said of God who is infinitely exalted above them all? The discussion is brought to an end by verses 31-33.

This, I repeat, is the first thing to which we are to humble ourselves. Let us lay our mouths in the dust and ourselves on the ground, and say, 'It is the Lord. I will be silent because he has done it. He is of one mind, and who can turn him? He does whatever he pleases. Am I not in his hand as clay in the hand of the potter? May he not make of me whatever kind of vessel he pleases? When I was not, he brought me out of nothing by his word. What I am, or have, is merely of his pleasure. O let my heart and thoughts be full of deep subjection to his supreme dominion and invincible sovereignty over me!' This is what brought peace to Aaron in his great distress, David in his (2 Sam. 15:25, 26), and Job in his. This truth is often presented by God (Jer. 10, Rom. 9:11, and many other places). If we intend to walk with God, we must submit ourselves to this, and in doing so, we shall find peace.

(ii) *His wisdom.* He is wise even as he speaks in derision of men's pretences at being wise. God alone is wise. He has resolved to make 'all things work together for good for those who love God' (Rom. 8:28); to ensure that we shall not be in any distress unless it is necessary (1 Pet. 1:6). But under many dispensations of his providence we find that we are at a loss; we cannot see how they can be understood as being in accordance with that rule. We do not see how this state or condition can be good for the church in general, or for us particularly. We imagine that it would bring more glory to God and more advantage to us if things were otherwise. The reasonings of the souls and hearts of men on this account are innumerable. We fail to appreciate how wicked are our thoughts on this subject. God wishes us to humble ourselves in all our circumstances and to bring our understandings captive before them (see Isa. 40:27, 28). This is where our hearts must rest when ready to complain: that his understanding is unsearchable; he sees all things in all their causes, effects and circumstances, to their utmost reach, tendencies and consequences. We walk in the shade, not knowing anything of what is before us. The day will come when we shall see every event in its context amongst all others, and infinite wisdom being displayed in them all. We will understand that all things were done in the right proportion of number, weight and measure; that nothing could have been disposed differently without the abridgement of the glory of God and of the good of his church. Indeed, I dare say that there is no saint of God presently distressed by some dispensation of providence, who, if he were, seriously and impartially, to consider his situation, the frame of his heart, his temptations and his ways, and so much of the aims and purposes of God that would certainly be revealed to faith and prayer, who would not discover some rays and beams of infinite wisdom shining through, tempered by love, goodness and faithfulness. But whether presently we have this light or are left in darkness, this is the haven and rest for our tossed souls, this the ark and bosom of our peace: for us to humble our souls under the infinite wisdom of God in all his procedures and on that basis quietly commit all things to his management.

(iii) *His righteousness.* Though God wishes us to acquiesce in his sovereignty when everything else is dark, yet he wishes us to realize also that all his ways are just and righteous. The holy God will do no iniquity. That he is righteous in all his ways and holy in all his works is declared as much as any other thing that he has revealed about himself. 'Shall the Judge of all the earth do what is right?' Is God unrighteous to inflict wrath on us? By no means! The righteousness of God – which springs from, and equates to, the universal rectitude of his nature, in respect of all his works – is infinite. I am speaking of that which is called '*Justitia regiminis,*' his ruling, or governing, righteousness as he dispenses rewards and punishments. Now because we are not able to discern it in the many paths of its working, it will help us in humbling ourselves before it to consider the following:

(a) God does not judge as man judges. Man judges by what is seen by the eye and heard by the ear, but God searches the heart. We know little of what is in the heart of men; the transactions that have taken place between God and them which, if they were revealed – as they shall be one day – would disclose the righteousness of God shining as the sun. Rest on this: we know so much less of the actions which God judges than we do of the rules by which he judges. Most things to him are different from what they seem to us.

(b) God is the great Judge of all the world, not of this place or that place. He therefore disposes all things for the good of the whole and to his universal glory. Our thoughts are bounded within a very narrow compass, and even more so our observations and knowledge. Something may seem deformed to us which, when viewed by one who sees it in its completeness, is full of beauty and order. One man may see only a small part of a statue and judge that it is distorted, while he who sees the whole may recognise its fine proportions and beauty. All things in all places, in past ages and in the future to come, lie naked and exposed before God, and he disposes of them in such a way that, in their contexts and relationships to one another, they shall be full of order. This is true righteousness.

(c) God judges here, not by any final, completed sentence, but by way of preparation for the judgment to come. This unties all knots and solves all difficulties. This shows forth the deepest distresses of the godly, and the highest advancements of wicked men, as righteous and beautiful. And in this truth let our souls rest in peace (Acts 17:29-31).

(d) God's goodness, kindness, love and tenderness. Our souls must humble themselves to believe that all these are to be found in God's dispensations. I will mention only that one reference where the apostle explains this, namely, Hebrews 12:1-6; adding also the words with which Hosea closes his description of God's various dealings and dispensations with his people (Hos. 14:9).

This is what is meant therefore by humbling our souls to the law of God's providence in all his dispensations. It is to fall down before his sovereignty, wisdom, righteousness, goodness, love and mercy. And without this frame of heart there is no walking with God. That is, unless we wish to come into his presence in order to quarrel with him, which would not be to our advantage.

This was Paul's attitude of heart. 'I have learnt it,' he says. 'It is not in me by nature, but I have now learnt it by faith (Phil. 4:11). I have humbled my soul to it, "in whatever situation." In every state and condition, good or bad, high or low, at liberty or in prison, respected or despised, in health or sickness, living or dying, I bow to the law of the good providence of God, in which is contentment.' It was the same with David (Psa. 131:1). He did not exercise or trouble himself with the ways and works of God which were too high and too hard for him. What, then, did he do? Part of his heart would have been speculating about these things, but he quietened himself and humbled his soul under God's providence (verse 2), with the comforting result that followed; namely, an exhortation not to dispute God's ways, but to hope and trust in him for the reasons mentioned (verse 3). This is also the advice given by James to believers in various situations (James 1:9, 10). Let everyone rejoice in God's ways towards them, willingly bowing their hearts to them.

This is a familiar truth, which we make use of daily. I could continue to discuss the reasons for it; its consequences, effects and advantages; its necessity, if we wish that God should have any glory, or our own souls any peace; the perfect conquest that will be obtained by it over the evils of any situation. And I could proceed to apply it to the saddest particular cases imaginable (for all of which the Scriptures are full of instruction) – but in doing so I would be digressing considerably.

This, then is the second thing to which we are to humble ourselves.

2. *There remains my last point: How, or by what means, are we to humble ourselves to the laws of grace and providence?*

I will look at just two of the principal graces which, when exercised, will fulfil this work.

(i) Let faith have its work. There are, among other things, two things that faith will do, and is suited to do, in this context:

(a) It empties the soul of self. This is the proper work of faith: to discover the utter emptiness, insufficiency, nothingness, that is in man for any spiritual work or purpose whatsoever (Eph. 2:8, 9). Faith is itself from God, not of ourselves, and it teaches us to depend, in everything, on grace and not on any works of our own. If we would wish to be something of ourselves, faith then tells us it has nothing for us, for it only fills those who are empty and, by grace, makes something only of those who are nothing of themselves. While faith is at work, it will fill the soul with thoughts like the following: I am nothing; a poor worm at

God's disposal; lost, if not found by Christ. I have done, can do, nothing for which I should be accepted by God. Surely God must be submitted to in all things and the way of his mere grace must be accepted' (Rom. 3:27). This is the proper work of faith: to exclude and shut out any boasting in self. That is, to reveal ourselves to us as those who have nothing to glory or rejoice in, of ourselves, so that God may be all in all. This working of faith will keep the heart ready to subject itself to God in all things, both in the law of grace and of providence.

(b) Faith will actually bring the soul to the foot of God's throne and give it up completely to his disposal. What did the faith of Abraham do when it obeyed the call of God (Isa. 41:2, KJV)? It brought him to the foot of God. God called him to be at his disposal completely, by faith to come to him, following him, he knew not where nor for what. 'Go from your kindred and your father's house,' and he does not argue. 'Cast out Ishmael, whom you love,' and Ishmael is gone. 'Sacrifice your own Isaac,' and he obeys. He was brought by faith to God's foot and waited there at his disposal for all things. This is the proper nature of faith: to bring a man to that condition. It was the same with David (2 Sam. 15:26). Faith will do this. Does God wish me to suffer in my name, estate, family? 'It is the Lord,' says faith. Does he wish me to be poor and despised in the world, of little or no use to him or to his people? 'Who,' says faith, 'will say to him: What are you doing?' In any state or condition faith will find arguments to keep the soul at God's disposal always.

(ii) *Constant, abiding reverence towards God* will help the soul in this universal resignation and humbling of itself.

This reverence of God is an awful, spiritual regard of the majesty of God, as he is pleased to concern himself with us and in our walking before him, on account of his holiness, greatness, omniscience and omnipotence (Heb. 12:28, 29; Psa. 89:7; 8:9).

A reverence for God arises from three things, as is seen in its description:

(a) The infinite excellence and majesty of God and his great name. This was the apostle's motive (Heb. 12:29; 4:13). See also Deuteronomy 28:58. God's excellence of itself not only makes wicked men and hypocrites tremble whenever the thought of it seizes them (Isa. 33:14), but it also fills the saints with dread and terror (Hab. 3:16). No one can bear the rays of his excellence, unless Christ shields them from us, allowing us to approach him with boldness.

(b) The infinite, inconceivable distance between us and God. This is the reason for the advice of the wise man to pay due regard to God at all times (Eccles. 5:2). He is in heaven, from where he reveals his glorious excellence in a poor worm creeping on the dust and clay of the earth, as we see in Abraham's example (Gen. 18:27). What an inconceivable distance there is between the glorious majesty of God and a little dust, on which the wind blows, and it is gone!

(c) This inconceivably glorious God is pleased, of his own grace, to condescend to concern himself with us, poor worms, and with our services, of which he stands in no need (Isa. 57:15). His eye is upon us; his heart is towards us. This causes David to break out in admiration (1 Chron. 17:16), and should do us also.

What advantages there are in maintaining a reverence to God in our hearts; in how many ways it enables us to humble our souls to the laws of his grace and providence; what an end it will put to all the opposing arguments of our hearts – I will not stop to consider. The use of the two graces, faith and reverence, is all that I shall presently recommend to you to help you fulfil this commandment that we are considering.

In our next sermon, I will arrive at that part of this whole series which is to be particularly emphasized.

Sermon 8

Walking Humbly with God (*cont.*)

And to walk humbly with your God.—Mic. 6:8

We have now considered fully the nature of this duty.

III. *We proceed to prove the first statement made and to conclude the whole.*

Humble walking with God is the great duty and the most precious concern of believers.

'What does the Lord require of you?' This is sufficiently stated in the text itself and, being so emphatically expressed, does not really need further confirmation. But because it is a truth that is found so often in Scripture, I will add a single proof for each part of the proposition, namely, that it is both our great duty, and our most precious concern.

For the former, consider the parallel reference of Deuteronomy 10:12, 13:

'What does the Lord your God require of you, but to fear the Lord your God, to walk in all his ways, to love him, to serve the Lord your God with all your heart and with all your soul, and to keep the commandments and statutes of the Lord, which I am commanding you today for your good?'

That which is expressed in my text as 'walking humbly with God' is here described more fully, but with exactly the same introduction: 'What does the Lord your God require of you?' This passage gives us both the root and the fruit. The root: in fear and love; the fruit: in walking in God's ways and keeping his commandments. The perfection in both is: to fear and love the Lord with all the heart and with all the soul; to walk in all his ways. This is the great thing that God requires from believers.

A similarly important reference with respect to the second point, the precious nature of this concern to believers, is found in the answer of the scribe which was commended by the Saviour: 'This is better than all your preaching, all your hearing, all your private meetings, all your conferences, all your fasting' (Mark 12:33). Whole burnt offerings and sacrifices were, at that time, the instituted worship of God, appointed by him and acceptable to him, as, presently, are the things which I have listed. But all these outward things may be copied; hypocrites may fulfil the outward form of them, as they in the past offered sacrifices. But walking humbly with God cannot be feigned. Nor are they, even in the best of men, of any value, other than as elements and fruits of humble walking. If under their cloak there lies, as might well be the case, a proud, unmortified heart, not subdued by the law of the Spirit of life, not humbled in all things to walk with God, both they and their performances are abhorred by God. Therefore, although all these elements of worship ought to be fulfilled, yet our great concern lies essentially in humble walking: 'Only let your manner of life be worthy of the gospel of Christ' (Phil. 1:27).

This is the significance of the expression at the beginning of the verse, 'What does the Lord your God require of you?' You may come up with other things in which you yourself find more delight, or which, you might believe, would be more acceptable to God. But do not be mistaken. This is the great thing that he requires of you: to walk humbly before him.

The reasons for it are these:

1. *Every person worries most about his own great purpose, whatever it might be.*

To achieve it, is what is most important to him; the great theme of his thoughts is whether he shall succeed in it. For a believer, the chief purpose is the glory of God. This is the case, or ought to be. This is the reason why they were created, for this they were redeemed and purchased, to be 'a people for his own possession.' Through all the Scriptures we are taught that the great means for glorifying God is by our humble walking with him, as is described to us: 'By this my Father is glorified, that you bear much fruit' (John 15:8). You may think that God is glorified by miracles and the like, that amaze and dazzle the eyes of the world. That may be so, but the highest glory to God arises from your bearing of much fruit. You know the general rule that our Saviour gave to his followers (Matt. 5:16). It is from our good works that men give glory to God. The same advice is repeated by the Holy Spirit in 1 Pet. 2:12.

There are various ways by which glory redounds to God from the humble walk of a believer:

(i) It gives him the glory of the doctrine of grace.

(ii) It gives him the glory of the power of grace.

(iii) It gives him the glory of the law of his grace: that he is a king who is obeyed.

(iv) It gives him the glory of the law of his justice.

(v) It gives him the glory of his kingdom: firstly, in its order and beauty; secondly, in the increase of his subjects.

(i) It gives God the glory of the doctrine of grace, or of the doctrine of the gospel, which is therefore called 'the glorious gospel of the blessed God' (1 Tim. 1:11), because it brings so much glory to him. If we walk according to this rule, we 'adorn the doctrine of God' (Titus 2:10). The apostle proceeds to explain what it is that the grace of God teaches us (Titus 2:11, 12), the substance of which is that we should walk humbly before God. And when men professing this grace walk according to its rule, it is rendered glorious. When the world sees that these are the fruits which that doctrine produces, they are forced to acknowledge it. Pride, folly and wickedness in believers have been the greatest obstacle that the gospel has ever received in the world. Nor will it be advanced, by the greatest efforts imaginable, until those who make the greatest profession of it are more conformed to it. The word is glorified when it 'speeds ahead and is honoured' (2 Thess. 3:1), which it will not do without the humble walk of believers. What great gifts are poured out in the days in which we live! What light is bestowed! What pains in preaching! How greatly is the word spread abroad! Yet how little ground is obtained! How few converted! The preaching of the word has free course, but it is not glorified by acceptable obedience. Is it not high time for believers to look to themselves, whether the obstacle does not lie in themselves? Don't we strengthen the world against the doctrine we profess by the fruits of it that they see in us and in our ways? Don't they say of us, 'These are our new lights and witnesses: proud, selfish, worldly, unrighteous; negligent of the commandments which they profess to honour; useless in their stations and generations; falling into the same ways which they condemn in others'? Perhaps they may take advantage falsely and maliciously of these things, but is it not high time for us to examine ourselves, in case, for all our preaching and talking, we have forgotten to walk humbly with God? In this way – not glorifying the gospel – have we hindered the free course of its work and efficacy?

(ii) Humble walking with God gives him the glory of the power of his grace – his converting, sanctifying grace. When the world sees a poor, proud, selfish, rebellious, fretful, perhaps immoral and coarse creature being made gentle, meek, humble, self-denying, sober and useful, they cannot but inquire after the secret and hidden virtue and power which produced such a change. This is what was stated as the glory of the grace that was to appear to men under the gospel: that it should change the nature of the vilest of men; that it should take away cruelty from the wolf and violence from the leopard, rage from the lion and poison from the asp, making them as gentle and useful as the kid, the calf, the lamb and the oxen (Isa. 11:6-9). It is not in our nature to humble ourselves to walk with God. We are opposed to it and everything to do with it. No angels or men can persuade us to it. Our carnal mind is enmity to him and not subject to his law, nor can it be. To have our souls humbled, brought to the foot of God, made always ready, willing, obedient, turned in their whole course, changed in all their ways and principles; this glorifies the grace of God which is dispensed in Christ and by which alone that work is wrought. When men profess to have received converting and renewing grace from God and separate themselves from the men of the world because of it, but then live as they do – or worse, so that their ways and walk are contemptible to all – this is the greatest reproach imaginable to that work of grace which they profess.

(iii) This gives God the glory of his law by which he requires obedience at our hand. The obedience of those who are subject to it sets forth the glory of the wisdom, goodness and power of the lawgiver who lies behind the law. This follows from my first point.

(iv) It gives him the glory of his justice, even in this world. There are two sorts of people in this world: the children of God and others. Both sorts are tempted with respect to each other. The children of God are often disturbed by the outward prosperity of the wicked; the men of the world are often disturbed by the public claim which Christians make of possessing the privilege of God's love and protection. 'Why them rather than others?' they ask. 'Or rather than ourselves?' For the first, we know those truths by which they are to quieten their hearts. For the latter, this is what gives God the glory of his justice, when those whom he owns in this world, who expect a crown of reward from him, are seen to walk humbly before him. 'Your steadfastness and faith in all your persecutions and afflictions,' says the apostle, 'is evidence of the righteous judgment of God, that you may be considered worthy of the kingdom of God'

(2 Thess. 1:4, 5). Their patient and humble walking will be the evidence to convince even the world of the righteous judgment of God, in rewarding them and rejecting itself. Though eternal life is the gift of God and has respect predominantly to the praise of his glorious grace in Jesus Christ, yet by intending to bestow it on us as a reward, he thereby manifestly glorifies his justice also. When men see those whom God will reward walking humbly before him, this gives a foretaste to them of his justice; revealing that his ways are just, and his judgment righteous, or, as the apostle expresses it, 'according to truth.'

(v) It gives him the glory of his kingdom, in being an effective means for the increase of the number of his subjects, and hence for the propagation of the kingdom in the world.

Now if by these, and by other truths which might be presented, it is seen that God is glorified more than anything else in this world by a humble walking before him, this humble walk must certainly be the greatest and incomparable concern of all those whose chief purpose is to advance God's glory.

2. It is our great concern because God is greatly delighted in it; it is well-pleasing to him.

The humble walk of believers is the great delight of God's soul, the one thing that he has in this world to delight him. If this is our aim, if this is our great interest – that we should please God, that he might delight in us and rejoice over us – then this is the way in which that must be done. 'As I dwell in the high and holy place; as I delight to abide in the heavens, where I manifest my glory,' says God, 'so also

I dwell, with delight and joy, with him who is of a contrite and lowly spirit' (Isa. 57:15). Men who are opposed to such a walk, whatever they might be in outward profession, are proud men. Nothing takes pride away in the sight of God but this humble walk with him. But 'the haughty he knows from afar' (Psa. 138:6). He takes notice of them, but with scorn and indignation. They are to him an abominable thing. It is solemnly asserted three times in the Scriptures that God resists the proud, or scorns the scorner, but gives grace to the humble and lowly (Prov. 3:34; James 4:6; 1 Pet. 5:5). God scorns, abominates, resists and sets himself against such men, but he gives grace, or favour, to the lowly, to the humble. This is wonderfully described by Isaiah (Isa. 66:1-3). There he is dealing with those who falsely profess faith; men who, in all that they did, said, 'Let the Lord be glorified' (verse 5). These men, aiming at acceptance with him and to have him delight in them, pretended two things in particular:

(i) To trust in the glory of the temple; that high and holy house that was built for God's own name. With respect to this, God says, 'Do you think that I have any need of it or any delight in it, though it is such a great and glorious building in your eyes? "Heaven is my throne, and the earth is my footstool. All these things my hand has made." What need do I have of the house that you have built, or what delight do I have in it?'

(ii) They trusted in their worship and service; the duties they performed in the temple – their sacrifices and oblations – praying, hearing. 'Alas,' said God. 'All these things I abhor.' He therefore compares them to the things his soul hates most, and which he had most sternly forbidden (verse 3). But if God does not take delight in any of these things; if neither temple or ordinances, worship or duty of religion, will prevail, what is it that he delights in? The Lord says, 'This is the one to whom I will look. I will rejoice over him and rest in my love.' Let the proud Pharisee come and boast of his righteousness, his duties, his worship and performances, but God's eye is on the poor creature behind the door, crying 'God be merciful to me, a sinner'; that is, giving himself up to sovereign mercy, and following after him on that basis. There is a holiness that puffs up, that in some men has little other fruit than, 'Stand away from me; I am holier than you.' God does not delight in this. It is hard to excel by humble walking. Distinction is so much more easily gained by other ways; but God does not delight in them.

(iii) It is our greatest concern because this alone is what makes us eminently conformable to Jesus Christ. When the church was raised up to expect his coming, she was told to look for him as one who is gentle and lowly (Zech. 9:9). And when he calls men to be conformed to his example, this is how he teaches them: 'Learn from me,' he says (Matt. 11:29). What shall we learn from him? What does he propose that we should imitate? That we should work miracles? Walk on the sea? Raise the dead? Speak as never man spoke? 'No,' he says. 'That is not your concern; but "learn from me, for I am gentle and lowly in heart, and you will find rest for your souls."' 'Have this mind among yourselves,' said the apostle, 'which is yours in Christ Jesus' (Phil. 2:5). What mind was this? He describes it in the next verse: Christ's humbling, emptying himself, making himself poor, making himself nothing, that he might do the will of God; coming to God's foot, waiting for his command; doing his will cheerfully and readily. 'Let this mind be in you,' he says. 'Be like Christ in this.' I could go over everything involved in humbly walking with God and show the excellence of Jesus Christ in it all, and how our conformity to Christ consists mainly in fulfilling this. But I must hasten on.

(iv) I could prove it further by investigating the promises that are made to those humbly walking with God. But this would be a long task, with many details to consider, so I will omit it entirely.

(v) It will be seen to be the case by comparing it with any other endeavour in which men consider that their interest and concern lie:

(a) Some men (I am speaking of professors of faith in Christ) live as though their greatest concerns were in heaping up to themselves the things of this world. Their hearts are devoured by their love for them and their thoughts taken up by them. I shall not even compare these worldly things with the humble walk before God, nor waste time in demonstrating their great inadequacy as true concerns for a believer, such is their vanity, uncertainty, uselessness as to our eternal end, and the lack of satisfaction, fear, and care which they bring with them.

(b) There are others whose desires are for greatness, high places, esteem in the world, longing to be somebody in their days; desires and longings which outstrip any call of providence and God to such appointments. They make

this their business and goal, without any further consideration. But we may say the same for these as for the former:
their way is folly, though their followers may praise their
words.

(c) There are those whose aim is to be truly learned, and so to
be esteemed. They make this their work. This, they believe,
is what will give them satisfaction. They give to it all their
time and strength. If they succeed in this, all is well: they will
have their hearts' desire. But the glory of this ambition is also
tarnished, and its vanity discovered; the shame of its naked-
ness has been revealed. Is this your great concern? Do you
waste your time and spirit over it? Is this where your hope
of rest lies? Have you laid up your glory here, and believe
that this is how you will obtain it at last? Poor creature! You
snuff up the empty wind. Throughout all this time, it may be
that God abhors you; your learning will never swell to such
a size that the door of hell will not be wide enough to receive
you. The vanity, frustration, dreadfulness, emptiness of this
endeavour may be easily discovered.

Say you gathered all these things together. Suppose
you had obtained high positions, great scholarship, and a
corresponding reputation and credit in them all; that you
had achieved all that your heart could desire and more
than any man before you. Would all of it give rest to your
soul? Can't you see through it all? Then why do you spend
your strength for something that is worthless? Why is the
flower of your spirit wasted on these things – things that are
nothing at all?

(d) Some men's great endeavours seem to lie in the profession of religion. It is enough for them to make a profession

and to obtain a reputation that they are believers. They are not concerned whether this humble walking with God, and all the causes and results of it, belongs to them. In order that men should not remain in this condition, let me add a few thoughts:

(1) Everything that they do may be imitated or counterfeited; therefore what benefit is it? It may be done by someone who does not have the least part of God or Christ in him. Hypocrites may hear much, pray often, speak of God and the things of God, perform all the duties of religion, excel in gifts and skills, gain a great name and reputation – and yet, still be hypocrites.

(2) All of this has been done by those who have perished. Many who are now in hell have done all these things and went down to the pit with the burden of the profession of faith and of their duties on their back. I could list examples. And let me lay this foundation (which I may safely do), that if all the excellencies that have been found in hypocrites and perishing souls be gathered together in one soul, yet he would still be a hypocrite, though possessing the best reputation that mere profession can obtain. Take the zeal of Jehu, the hearing of Herod, the praying of the Pharisee, the fasting of the Jews (Isa. 58), the joy of the stony ground, and you could dress up a perishing soul to a degree of professing faith beyond what most of us arrive at.

(3) It is of no use in this world. I can confidently say, take away this humble walking, and all profession of faith is nothing. It does no good at all in the world. Is it of any advantage to mankind that a man should obtain a

reputation for his religion, but cannot relate one instance that any man, high or low, rich or poor, had been the better for his existence in the world? That those who should do good to all, in fact do good to none at all? Is this what is meant by being fruitful in the gospel? Is this the performing of good works that are profitable to all? Is this to do good to mankind in those circumstances in which we are placed?

(4) This is the easiest way for a man to deceive himself to eternity. If any wishes to go down to the pit in peace, let him maintain worship in the family and in private; let him listen to sermons as often as he has the opportunity; let him speak of good things; let him forsake the company of profane and ignorant people, until he has obtained a great reputation for religion. Let him preach and labour to make others better than himself. And if, in the meantime, he neglects to humble his heart to walk with God in evident holiness and usefulness, he will not fail in his purpose.

Do not mistake my meaning. Far be it that I should encourage profane men in their contempt of God's ways and in their accusations of hypocrisy that they are so ready to throw at the best of God's saints. Far be it, I say. Nor let me be interpreted in the least as pleading for men who satisfy themselves in a righteousness which does not possess these works. I consider them as men who are wholly ignorant of the mystery of God, and of the Father, and of Christ, and clearly not interested in the covenant of grace. No, what I aim at is this: I would not have professors of faith flatter themselves in a vain, empty profession, when the fruits they demonstrate of envy, hatred, pride and folly proclaim that their hearts are not humbled to walk with God. Can such men, or any of these vain efforts, ever stand in competition with what I have proposed as the greatest concern of men? In comparison to it, they are, without doubt, nothing.

Application 1

Is humble walking with God our great concern? Let us make it our business and our work to bring our hearts to it throughout our days. What are we doing, running around all day long, spending our strength for that which is not bread? My business is not whether I shall be rich or poor, wise or foolish, learned or ignorant; whether I shall live or die; whether there will be peace or war with the nations; whether my family shall flourish or wither; whether my gifts shall be many or few, great or small; whether I have a good or a bad reputation in the world; but only whether I walk humbly with God or not. My present condition can be judged only with respect to this, as will my future acceptance. I have tired myself in chasing many things, but this is the one thing necessary. What does God require of me other than this? What does all the sanctifying work of the Holy Spirit tend to, other than that I should walk humbly with God?

Allow me to present two or three motives for our help and encouragement:

(i) In humble walking with God we shall find peace in all circumstances: 'Learn from me, for I am gentle and lowly in heart, and you will find rest for your souls' (John 11:29). 'Let war come upon the country; I shall have peace. Let my financial position collapse; I shall have peace. Let my nearest relations be taken away; I shall have peace.' The soul that seeks its rest, and makes it its great concern to walk humbly before God, is brought to God's foot, submits to his will, is prepared for his disposal. Whatever God does in the world with himself, with his possessions, or with others, he has peace and quietness in it. His own will is gone; the will of God is his choice. His one great concern does not lie in anything that can perish or be lost.

(ii) We shall also find comfort. Mephibosheth said: 'Oh, let him take it all, since my lord the king has come safely home' (2 Sam. 19:30). When a man shall see that, even in his worst state and circumstances, his great concern is safe, that it can never be taken away from him, it fills his heart with delight. Is he prosperous? He does not fear the loss of that which he values most. Is he in adversity? Yet he can still walk with God, which is all in all to him. He can therefore glory in tribulations, rejoice in afflictions; his treasure, his main concern, is safe.

(iii) Only this will make us useful in our generation and fruitful in the knowledge of our Lord and Saviour Jesus Christ. All the glory we bring to God and all the good that we do to men depends on this.

If we make this our business – if we aim at it, in Christ's strength – we shall find peace in it.

Application 2

To humble us all – we who have spent so much of our time and days in things which, in reality, concern us so little – let us judge our ways and affairs by the balance of the sanctuary. We rise early, go to bed late, and wear ourselves out so as to increase knowledge and learning. What have we achieved when all is done? A tool in Satan's hand to puff us up with pride and folly, a distraction from the knowledge of Christ, a striving after wind. How many other things have entangled us! What importance have we placed upon them! How we have valued that profession of faith which has been more of a shame rather than an honour to the gospel! The Lord forgive us our folly in spending ourselves in things with which we have so little concern; may he help us so that our mistake will not prove fatal at last. If we could only review our lives seriously and realise how much time we have spent on things that, in reality, do us no good, it would certainly fill our souls with a great deal of shame and confusion.

Application 3

As for those who are not in any way concerned with this matter, who have never in their lives sought to walk with God, let me say to such:

(i) It is more than probable that they will take advantage of what has been said against empty professors and professions. In their minds they will triumph over them, and say, 'This is exactly what they are like; they are no better than this.' If so, it is possible that these sermons, through the just judgment of God, will tend to harden them further in their sin, pride and folly. What the Lord's intentions towards you are, I do not know. It is my duty to warn you of this. Some of those who profess faith may, indeed, fail to attain the mark of our high calling, but you who have no profession will never attain it. Take great care that this should not be the consequence of the preaching of this word to you. I would prefer never to preach again at this place than to speak one word with the purpose of giving you an advantage against those who profess faith. If you take it, it will be your ruin.

(ii) Consider this: if the righteous are scarcely saved, where will you be? And those like you, bitter scoffers, those who neglect the ordinances, haters of the powers of godliness and the purity of religion. You, whose pride and folly, or whose formality, lukewarmness and superstition, whose company and society, whose ways and daily walk demonstrate that you are complete strangers to this great concern of believers. I ask you: What will be your doom and portion?

(iii) Consider how useless you are in this world. You bring no glory to God, but only dishonour. By your outward acts you may suppose that you sometimes do good to men, but you can be certain that you truly do more harm, every day, than any good done by you throughout your lives. How many, by you, are drawn into hell! How many are hardened! How many are destroyed by living in empty formality or profane unbelief!

Sermon 9

God, the Saints' Rock[1]

From the end of the earth I call to you when my heart is faint. Lead me to the rock that is higher than I.—Psa. 61:2

THERE are two things in these words: First, the state in which the psalmist found himself; second, the course that he steered in that state.

I. His state is expressed in two ways: 1. The place where he found himself: 'From the end of the earth'; and 2. The condition he was in: 'my heart is faint' ('overwhelmed,' KJV).

II. The course that he steers also involves two things: 1. Its manner: 'He called to the Lord'; 2. The content of his call: 'Lead me to the rock that is higher than I.'

I. *Firstly, we consider his state.*

1. The first description of it (both descriptions are metaphorical) refers to the place where he found himself: 'the end of the earth.' This could be understood in two ways: either naturally, in which case it refers to men who are far away from help, relief and comfort; or (in an ecclesiastical sense) referring to God's temple, which was *in*

[1] Preached on 11 November, 1670.

medio terrae (in the midst and heart of the land), where God manifested and gave evident signs of his gracious presence. It is as if he had said, 'I am at the end of the earth, far from any tokens, pledges or manifestations of the love and favour of God, as well as from any outward help and assistance.'

2. The second description of his state is that 'his heart was faint,' in which there are two things to note:

(i) A convergence of calamities and distresses.

(ii) The effect they had upon him: his heart was over-whelmed and faint under them. As long as the heart holds up these may be borne. 'A man's spirit will endure sickness' (Prov. 18:14), but when the spirit is wounded and the heart faints, overwhelming calamities can oppress and overcome.

In Psalm 102, David expands on what he means here by 'faint.' The title of this psalm is 'A prayer of one afflicted, when he is faint,' and he describes that condition (verses 3-10):

> My days pass away like smoke, and my bones burn like a furnace.
> My heart is struck down like grass and has withered; I forget to eat my bread.
> Because of my loud groaning my bones cling to my flesh.
> I am like a desert owl of the wilderness, like an owl of the waste places;
> I lie awake; I am like a lonely sparrow on the housetop.
> All the day my enemies taunt me; those who deride me use my name for a curse.

> For I eat ashes like bread and mingle tears with my
>   drink, because of your indignation and anger;
> For you have taken me up and thrown me down.

To be overwhelmed is to be buried under all kinds of
trouble. David provides another description in Psalm 142
(verses 3, 4):

> When my spirit faints within me, you know my way!
> In the path where I walk they have hidden a trap for me.
> Look to the right and see: there is none who takes notice
>   of me;
> No refuge remains to me; no one cares for my soul.

To have a heart that is faint is therefore to be overwhelmed
by a mass of various troubles and an awareness that God's
indignation is the source of those troubles, so that the spirit
sinks and faints beneath its load. This is the psalmist's state
and condition.

II. *Secondly, the course he takes in this state has two
elements, as we have already observed.*

1. The manner of it: 'I call to you.' This phrase is often used
in Scripture in this context, and it is a natural expression of
the action of faith in a distressed condition.

There are four ways in which the believer's faith will
act when he is in distress; all of them are involved in the
expression 'I call.'

(i) Faith makes the heart aware of its affliction. God abhors
the proud and the stubborn who think that by their own
spirits they can bear up under pressure. 'Listen to me, you
stubborn of heart, you who are far from righteousness' (Isa.
46:12). People who think that they can uphold themselves

by strength of heart when God is dealing with them are those who, above all others, are despised and abhorred by God. They are 'far from righteousness.' Calling involves an acknowledgement of the evils and distresses afflicting the spirit and does not despise God when we are chastened. It shows also that we have not utterly fainted but can still cry to him.

(ii) The next act of faith, when so distressed, is a holy complaint to God. David mentioned this: 'A prayer of one afflicted, when he is faint and pours out his complaint before the Lord.' He often mentions 'his complaint,' 'coming with his complaint to the Lord.' There is nothing that God responds to with more kindness than when we come with our complaints to him; not fretting in discontent but spreading our complaints before the Lord, from whom alone we expect relief. This shows that we believe that God is concerned with our state and condition. No one is so foolish, whatever he is suffering, as to complain to someone whom he does not believe is concerned about him or has any compassion for him. When we cry to God and pour out our complaints before him, it is an acknowledgement to him that we believe that he is concerned for our condition.

(iii) In this act of calling there is an effort made to approach to God, just as there is when you cry to someone who is some distance away and you are afraid that he will move further away from you. It is the great work of faith to call out to God when he is far off and you are afraid that at the next turn will be completely out of sight. Calling on God implies that he is withdrawing or departing.

[174]

(iv) There is a seriousness about it. It expresses the greatest determination of spirit that we possess, when we call out to God in any situation.

This is how the psalmist behaves in these circumstances: he has a sense of his distress, he complains to the Lord, he calls out after him in case he should withdraw himself. He does so with determination, in the hope that God would come to his help.

2. The content of his call is that God might 'lead him to the rock.' That is, that God would grant him an access to himself by Jesus Christ, in whom God is our rock and refuge in all distresses. He cries that God might open a way through all his dark and overwhelming difficulties; that he might approach him and spread out before him all the troubles and perplexities that have waylaid him.

What I wish to speak to you from these words is the following:

Observation

In the most overwhelming, disastrous afflictions that may befall a believing soul, faith still keeps its eye on God's store of grace and delights to break through all its troubles and to approach him; though, at the same time, it acknowledges that God is the author of all these afflictions.

I have already mentioned what I mean by these afflictions. There are two sorts: internal and external.

1. *Internal afflictions are those that arise from the perplexities of soul and conscience because of sin.* When the soul is in darkness and has no sense of any foundation upon which it

might find acceptance with God; when it is pressed with the guilt of sin and dwells in darkness because of this, having no light.

2. *External afflictions are of two kinds.*

(i) *Private.* In afflictions, losses, sickness, pains, and poverty, our own or of those who are dear to us, for whom we are concerned. They may sometimes have such an edge to them that they become overwhelming.

(ii) *Public.* With regard to God's church, when that is in great distress, without any prospect of relief or ray of light; when the summer is past and the harvest ended; when hopes have come to a head, but no relief ensues. When Zion is in the dust and the bones of Zion's children lie scattered like wood upon the face of the earth. Here is an overwhelming distress for those whose hearts are in God's ways and who have a concern for his glory.

These are the elements of overwhelming distresses. And faith, I say, perceives them as proceeding from God. Is the soul in distress because of sin? This is God's rebuke, God's arrows. It is God that caused this darkness. Is it troubled or pressed because of afflictions or dangers? 'Affliction,' says faith, 'does not spring up out of the earth, or troubles from the ground; these things are from God.' Is it a distress arising from the condition of the church of God? 'Who gave up Jacob to the looter, and Israel to the plunderers?' Is it not the Lord, he against whom we have sinned? It is therefore his wrath and his indignation that we see in all these things. Yet, notwithstanding all this, faith will look through all and find relief in God himself.

I shall:

I. Give some examples of this.

II. Show the basis of it.

III. Emphasize my main point; namely, discovering what it is in God that, in such overwhelming conditions, faith sees and fixes upon, in order to find support and relief.

IV. Show how this differs from that general hope in God which natural man is prone to depend on when in distress.

I. *Some examples*

We have a very remarkable example in the case of Jonah, who tells us that he was in 'the belly of Sheol' (Jonah 2:2; 'the belly of hell,' KJV). Sheol (hell), in Scripture, when it is applied to the things of this world, refers to the depth of temporal evils. 'The cords of death encompassed me ... the cords of Sheol entangled me,' says David (Psa. 18:4, 5), when he was speaking of the time of his affliction and persecution under Saul. And the 'belly of Sheol' must be the darkness and confusion of all those calamitous distresses. What did Jonah believe was the source of all these? He tells us, 'You cast me into the deep' (Jon. 2:3). He knew that the reason for it was his own sinful rebellion, but he refers it all to the principal cause: God himself. 'You cast me into the deep.' And how did this affect him? 'My life was fainting away' (verse 7). What relief did he then have? 'The waters closed in over me to take my life; the deep surrounded me; weeds were wrapped about my head at the roots of the mountains. I went down to the land whose bars closed upon me for ever' (verses 5, 6). No kind of relief, support, or succour was to be expected. What did he do? He tells us: 'My prayer came to you, into your holy temple' (verse 7). His eye was upon God, the one who had thrown him into this situation.

David gives us several instances of such occasions in his life. Once, I admit, he was mistaken in the action he took. He tells us so himself. He had described the overwhelming condition in which he was found (Psa. 55:3-5). And what was his response? 'Oh, that I had wings like a dove! I would fly away and be at rest; yes, I would wander far away; I would lodge in the wilderness' (verses 6, 7). 'Oh, that I could leave all these perplexities; that I was rid of these who are ready to overwhelm me!' But this was not the right course. I could give innumerable examples of a better response. Psalm 31:9-13 is a description of as sad a condition as any man can fall into, and which is accompanied by a great sense of God's displeasure, and of his own sin. 'My strength fails because of my iniquity, and my bones waste away' (verse 10). What was his response in this case? 'But I trust in you, O Lord; I say, "You are my God"' (verse 14). 'When my strength failed because of my iniquities, and my bones wasted away; when there was nothing but distress around me, and that from God, yet then I trusted in you, and I said, "You are my God."' And this is what God invites us to do.

Jacob complained: 'My way is hidden from the Lord, and my right is disregarded by my God' (Isa. 40:27). As professors of the gospel there are only two things that concern us in this world.

Firstly, our 'way'; that is, the course of obedience and profession in which we are engaged, according to the truth. In this sense, believing in Christ is called a 'way.' 'My way of faith, my way of worship, my way of obedience is disregarded by my God; God takes no notice of it.' This is equivalent to saying, 'My all, in the things of God, is at a loss; God takes no notice of my way.' If that is truly our condition, we are of all men most miserable.

There is also our 'right,' or 'judgment' (KJV); that is, the judgment that is to be passed upon our cause and way. It is what David so often prays about when he begs that God would 'judge him in his righteousness.' The church, here, is saying, 'God takes no notice of me and has disregarded my cause in the world. My judgment is passed over, not determined for me anymore; instead, he lets me suffer under the judgment of the world.' When our way and judgment are passed over – when our way and obedience seem hidden from God – God is indeed taking no notice of them. When he relinquishes the judgment and determination of our cause, what have we left in the world? But what does God now propose to Jacob, to the church, for their relief? What promises, what encouragements will he remind them of? Nothing, apart from himself. 'Have you not known? Have you not heard? The Lord is the everlasting God, the Creator of the ends of the earth. He does not grow faint or grow weary; his understanding is unsearchable' (Isa. 40:28). God calls upon them to consider him in his own nature and being, and in all his glorious acts. He calls upon our faith to look for rest in him alone. It is impossible that your way and right should be disregarded by him because he is 'the everlasting God,' the Lord, the Creator.

II. *We come now to the basis for this; why is it that faith looks for rest in him alone?*

It does so for two reasons:

1. It knows how to distinguish between the nature of the covenant and its external administration.

2. It is natural for faith to do so, for two reasons, as we shall presently see.

1. *Faith looks for rest in God because it is able to distinguish between the covenant itself, which is firm, stable, and invariable, and the administration of the covenant, which is variable and changeable.* I am referring to the outward administration of the covenant. God teaches us this in Psalm 89:30-34: 'If his children' (that is, the children of Jesus Christ) 'forsake my law and do not walk according to my rules, if they violate my statutes and do not keep my commandments, then I will punish their transgression with the rod and their iniquity with stripes, but I will not remove from him my steadfast love or be false to my faithfulness. I will not violate my covenant or alter the word that went forth from my lips.' The covenant of God, therefore, stands firm and unalterable, even when the rod and stripes of men are upon our backs. Amongst all the visitations of God because of sin, whether due to internal rebukes or outward chastisements, faith sees the stability of the covenant, and responds to God on that account. When David came to die, he summarised his experience of the immutability of the covenant, for all the changeableness of its outward administration: 'Although my house be not so with God, yet he hath made with me an everlasting covenant, ordered in all things and sure' (2 Sam. 23:5, KJV). 'In whatever way God deals with my house, whatever misery is brought upon us, yet the covenant itself is everlasting, ordered in all things and sure.' Whatever misery and distress may fall upon a believing soul (and I pray to God that he will help me to believe this, as well as to say it); whatever darkness or temptation

may befall him because of sin; whatever pressure, due to afflictions, persecutions, dangers, may arise; they all belong to God's covenant dispensations in dealing with him. God, being a God in covenant, will act according to his covenant in all things.

Hezekiah states: 'O Lord, by these things men live, and in all these is the life of my spirit' (Isa. 38:16). What things is he speaking of? 'Why,' he says, 'like a lion he breaks all my bones; from day to night you bring me to an end … What shall I say? For he has spoken to me, and he himself has done it. I walk slowly all my years because of the bitterness of my soul' (Isa. 38:13-15). One would think that his next words would be, 'By these things men die.' But no, he says, 'By these things believers live, and in these is the life of my soul,' because they are all administered from the unchanging covenant for the good of those souls who are exercised by them. In these dispensations of his providence, according to the degree to which God has been pleased to reveal himself, so also to that same degree the soul is to think of God. Does God hide his face and leave the soul to darkness? In darkness it must be. 'When he is quiet, who can condemn? When he hides his face, who can behold him?' (Job 34:29). Whether it is done to a nation or to one man only; whether it is against one person or the whole church of God; if he hides his face and causes darkness, no one can behold him. When God chastens us, we cannot think of him other than as angry; when he gives us up into the hands of men, hard masters, we cannot but consider it as a sign of his displeasure. When God acts in this way in the outward dispensation of his covenant, so that all things are dark and express his displeasure, and we are brought to view him as a God who hides himself and is displeased with us, exercising his anger against us; in such a day what then is the soul to do? Under all these tokens of God's displeasure, faith, although weak and faint, will work through to God himself, as one who is unchangeable in his covenant, and there find a supply in him surpassing all. 'Clouds and thick darkness are all round him; righteousness and justice are the foundation of his throne' (Psa. 97:2). 'I confess that I am surrounded by clouds and darkness, but if I could only break through these clouds, the results of God hiding his face, and come to his throne, there is righteousness and justice. That righteousness and justice by which he has betrothed me to himself by covenant' (Hos. 2:19, KJV). 'Could I get through this darkness of mind, this pressure upon my spirit, this sense of guilt, and come to his throne, there I would find him faithful and sure in all his promises, and immutable in his love.'

Suppose someone has all these troubles upon him at once; that God has left him under a great sense of sin (for our troubles about sin are not according to the greatness of our sin, but according to the sense of them that God plants in us, and those who are most troubled because of their sin are not to be thought of as the greatest sinners) and his difficulties are very great. And at the same time the Lord, in his providence, is pleased to exercise him with sharp afflictions. And if, at the same time, his interest and concern for the people of God is so troubled and distressed that there is no relief for him there either. For such a person there are clouds and darkness all around God. What will faith do in such a case? True faith will secretly work, through everything, to the throne of God, where there is righteousness and justice and acceptance with him. It is therefore said, 'I will wait for the Lord, who is hiding his face from the house of Jacob, and I will hope in him' (Isa. 8:17). The face of God is his love in Christ and the shining of his countenance in the promises of the covenant, for the way by which God communicates his love to our hearts is by his promises. Now, when the soul is sensible of no communication of love, nor promise of it, then God is said to hide his face. What will faith do in such a situation? Take itself somewhere else for relief? 'No,' it says, 'I will wait for the Lord, who is hiding his face.' Like a traveller, when the sky is full of clouds and darkness ready to break upon him, but who remembers that these are only interruptions, and that the sun is still where it was, and that if he can only shelter until the storm is over it will shine out again and its beams refresh him, so it is with the soul in this case. It remembers that God is still where he was. 'Though there are clouds within and distresses without – sorrow and anguish and fears round about, and the enemy entering into the very soul – yet the sun is still where it was. God will hide us where we may wait until this indignation is over and the light of his countenance will again shine upon me.' Faith views God, in the midst of all his varying providences, and so finds relief.

2. *This is the natural way for faith to act, as it is the principle of the new nature that is inside us that came from God, and will draw near to God whatever difficulties lie in the way.*

Evangelical faith has a secret double attraction towards God:

(i) Because of that innate respect which it necessarily and autonomously has towards Jesus Christ. Being the purchase of Christ, wrought in us by his Spirit, and being the product and issue of Christ's anguish, it has a natural tendency towards him. 'Who through him are believers in God' (1 Pet. 1:21); through Christ as mediator, as our surety, undertaking for us. Whatever therefore may overwhelm the soul, where there is the least faith, it will find relief in this: that Christ was substituted in its place against all the real indignation and wrath of God. The father of the faithful was once reduced to great distress, when he lifted his knife to the throat of his only son. But when destruction lay so near to the door, a voice called to him from heaven and stopped him, and he looked behind him and saw a ram caught for a sacrifice to God. When many a poor soul has the knife at the throat of all his consolations, ready to die, he hears a voice behind him that makes him look and see Christ provided for him, as a substitute in his place.

(ii) The new creature is the child of God, in whom faith is the main principle. It is begotten in him of God, of his own will; and so, against all obstacles and difficulties whatsoever, it is drawn to him.

III. *I now proceed to consider what it is that faith, in such overwhelming situations as I have described, sees in God to give it support and relief, that it should not be utterly swallowed up.*

1. *The first thing that faith considers, in such a condition, is the nature of God and his glories.* This is what God, in the first place, offers for our relief: 'I will not execute my burning anger; I will not again destroy Ephraim.' What reason does he give to assure us that he will not do this? 'For I am God and not a man, the Holy One in your midst' (Hos. 11:9). He

presents his own nature to faith's view, to confirm us that whatever our expectations might be, he will not execute the fierceness of his wrath; and he reproaches those who will put their trust in anything that is not God. 'They have made me jealous with what is no god' (Deut. 32:21). And he curses him 'who trusts in man and makes flesh his strength' (Jer. 17:5). He presents himself for our trust: one of infinite goodness, grace, bounty and patience.

There are two ways in which God presents his nature for our consideration, so as to relieve our faith when in overwhelming distress:

(i) He presents *his name*. The name of God is God himself: 'Those who know your name put their trust in you' (Psa. 9:10); that is, 'They know you.' Whatever the name might signify, it is the nature of God that is declared by it. And you know how he invites and encourages us to trust in the name of God: 'The name of the Lord is a strong tower; the righteous man runs into it and is safe' (Prov. 18:10). 'Let him … trust in the name of the Lord and rely on his God' (Isa. 50:10). The name of the Lord is what he declares himself to be: 'The Lord, a God merciful and gracious, slow to anger, and abounding in steadfast love and faithfulness … forgiving iniquity and transgression and sin' (Exod. 34:6, 7). Here he reveals and declares his name. God offers his name and its declaration in opposition to the working of unbelief. The effect of unbelief is an apprehension that God is severe and wrathful; that he watches for our mistakes, treasures up every failing and sin so as to avenge himself upon them, and that he will do so in fury. No, says God, 'Fury is not in me' (Isa. 27:4, KJV). The Lord is good and gracious; this is seen in his name, especially as it is revealed in Christ, so that faith will find secret encouragement in it in all distresses.

In passing, you may observe from this how that God, in former days while the work of revelation was still in progress and he was declaring himself little by little, still gave out his name as the state and condition of the church and his people required. He continually called on them to trust in his name. How did he reveal himself to Abraham? He tells us, 'I appeared to Abraham ... as God Almighty' (Exod. 6:3). In the account of this (Gen. 17:1) we read that he told Abraham: 'I am God Almighty.' He also gave him an explanation of that name: 'I am thy shield, and thy exceeding great reward' (Gen. 15:1, KJV). Abraham's condition was such that he had no protection in the world; he was a stranger and he wandered up and down among strange nations that were stronger than he. In this situation he might have feared destruction every day. 'Fear not,' God said, 'for I am God Almighty. I am your shield.' With faith in this, Abraham travelled among the nations. At that time, he had no child. What purpose, therefore, was there in all his travelling? 'Why,' said God, 'I am your reward.'

Again, in Genesis 14, where we read of the nations of the world beginning to fall into idolatry, Melchizedek is called the 'priest of God Most High.' God revealed himself to be a 'high God' so as to cast contempt upon their dunghill gods. And when Abraham came to speak to the king of Sodom, he said, 'I have sworn by the most-high God.' When God came to bring his people out of Egypt, he revealed himself to them by the name Jehovah. 'I did not reveal myself by this name previously,' he said, 'but now I do so because I have come to substantiate my promise.' In this way God

GOD, THE SAINTS' ROCK

dealt with his church, when coming to maintain it, by a
progressive revelation. But now he reveals himself by his
complete name, and we may take to ourselves whatever is
best suited to our distress. In particular, we may use that
name which includes all the rest: 'The God and Father of
our Lord Jesus Christ.'

(ii) *God reveals his nature by comparing himself to such creatures that act out of natural kindness*: 'Can a woman forget
her nursing child? Yet I will not forget you.'

There are three reasons why it is necessary that faith, in an
overwhelming situation, should have regard to the nature of
God and the essential properties of his nature, for its relief:

(a) Because of the circumstances of our distress;
(b) Because of their nature;
(c) Because of the nature of faith.

(a) *Because of the circumstances of our distress.* There are
three or four distressing circumstances that might befall us
against which faith can obtain no relief other than from the
essential properties of God's nature.

(1) *The first is that of place.* Believers may be brought into
distress anywhere in the world: in a lions' den, with Daniel;
in a dungeon, with Jeremiah; they may be banished to
the ends of the world, as John to Patmos; or they may be
driven into the wilderness, as the woman by the fury of the
dragon. The whole church may be thrown into places where
no eye can see them, and no hand relieve them, where no
one knows whether they are among the living or the dead.
What can give support to God's people when they fall into
such distresses as these? Only what Jeremiah tells us: 'Am I
a God at hand, declares the Lord, and not a God afar off, to

the ends of the earth' (Jer. 23:23)? 'Where shall I flee from your presence? … to the uttermost parts of the sea?' (Psa. 139:7). It is all in vain; the essential omnipresence of God is the only thing that can relieve the souls of believers against these great distresses of being driven to various places, suffering afflictions, and being overwhelmed by them. If the world could cast us out where God cannot be found and is not present, how it would triumph! It was part of the people's bondage and difficulties of old that the worship of God was confined to one specific country and place, so that when their enemies exiled them from that land they had the right, as it were, to command them, 'Go, serve other gods.' God has removed that bondage; all the world cannot exile us to a place where we cannot worship him. Wherever there are holy people, there is a holy land, and we cannot be driven into any land where God cannot be found. If we should be forced to leave our country, we have no reason to fear that we shall leave our God behind. God's essential omnipresence is a great relief against such circumstances, especially to souls who are cast out where no eye can pity them. Should they be thrown into dungeons, like Jeremiah, yet they can say, 'God is here.'

(2) *Similarly with respect to time*. The sufferings of the church of God are not tied down to one age or generation. 'We can see a little comfort and relief that may continue for our own days, but what will become of our posterity in future ages?' Why, God's immutability is the same through-out all generations! 'His loving-kindness fails not,' as the psalmist tells us, and this is the only relief against such distress. Alas, if a man should measure the prospects of

the church in the world, as they seem today, and notice the advance of wickedness like a flood in all parts of the world, he might be ready to think, 'What will God do for his great name? What will become of the gospel in another age?' But God is the same through all times and ages.

(3) *There is a relief to be found in God, and only in him, when everything is lost, and nothing remains.* If a man loses his lands, but his house remains, he has some relief; he knows where to lay his head, with all its cares. But when everything is gone, what can relieve him? Nothing but God and his all-sufficiency. This was Habakkuk's comfort at the thought that everything might fail him: 'Yet,' he said, 'I will rejoice in the Lord; I will take joy in the God of my salvation.'

(4) *The last circumstance of distress is death.* We do not know the details of how it will come upon us; we do not know how soon this will be. When all our present state and frame shall vanish and we find ourselves completely withdrawn from all things below; when the curtain will be drawn aside and we shall look into another world, the soul's relief will be in God's immutability. We shall find him the same towards us in death as he was in life, and much more.

Sermon 10

God, the Saints' Rock (*cont.*)[1]

*From the end of the earth I call to you when my heart is
faint. Lead me to the rock that is higher than I.*—Psa. 61:2

In my previous sermon on this text, I told you that there
were three reasons why faith looks to God's nature for relief
in overwhelming distresses. The first reason was found in
the circumstances of those distresses; the second in their
nature; and the third in the nature of faith itself. I dealt, in
that sermon, with the first of these reasons, and I shall now
proceed to the second.

(b) There are some distresses, because of their nature, that
refuse all the relief that you can offer to them other than
what may be found in the fountain itself: the nature of God.
Zion's distress described in Isaiah 49:14 is a case in point:
'But Zion said, "The Lord has forsaken me; my Lord has
forgotten me."' Or 40:27: 'My way is hidden from the Lord,
and my right is disregarded by my God.' She was in such
distress that nothing but the thought of God's nature could
give her relief. God therefore declared to her, 'Have you not

---

[1] Preached on 25 November, 1670.

known? Have you not heard? The Lord is the everlasting God, the Creator of the ends of the earth. He does not faint or grow weary' (Isa. 40:28). One might think that it would not be very difficult to answer all those objections which believing souls raise against themselves, particularly those of whom we are well assured are believers. But the opposite is often the case, and nothing will resolve their doubts other than a consideration of the infinite grace and goodness that is in God.

There may even be temporal troubles which, because of their nature, fail to be relieved by any other means. Think of when the whole church of God finds itself in such extreme circumstances in the world that nothing can alleviate it except infinite power, goodness and wisdom. You know how Moses was embarrassed when God told him that he would deliver Israel out of Egypt. Moses thought this was impossible and he continued to raise objections until he asked, 'If that must be the case, tell me *your name*' (Exod. 3:13). Until God reassured him by declaring his name – that is, his nature – Moses could not see any possible way for the church to be delivered. And we can find ourselves in the same situation as Moses. When God did not reveal himself, Moses thought that he could deliver Israel himself, and he went and killed an Egyptian; but when God did appear, Moses could not believe that he could do it, until he revealed his name.

But some might object: 'When faith approaches God to find relief, and God declares himself, faith will find other things in him as well as his goodness, grace and mercy. There is severity, justice, and righteousness in God, which will produce just as much discouragement on the one hand as the encouragement produced by different attributes on the other. To come to God and see him glorious in holiness and infinite in severity and righteousness – this would be a discouragement.'

I will answer this briefly and then proceed:

(1) It is very true that God is so. He is no less infinitely holy than infinitely patient and condescending; no less infinitely righteous than infinitely merciful and gracious. But these properties of God's nature shall not be immediately glorified upon those who go to him and address him by faith, though that will be the case for others. Only faith can obtain a proper view of God. Wicked men's thoughts are of two kinds. *Firstly*, they think wickedly, 'That God is one like themselves' (Psa. 50:21). Under the power of their corruptions and temptations and pursuing their lusts, they have no other thought of God but this. What they mean is that God is not very angry with them for their behaviour but cares for them, in their sins, just as he does for the holiest in the land. *Secondly*, their other thoughts (usually when it is too late, and God sends his terrors into their souls) are as the prophet Isaiah describes: 'Who among us can dwell with everlasting burnings?'

(2) God has given believers an assurance that he will not deal with them according to the strictness of his holiness and the severity of his justice. We consider Job, who said, 'Oh, that I knew where I might find him, that I might come even to his seat! I would lay my case before him and fill my mouth with arguments' (Job 23:3, 4). But does he know of whom he is speaking? And what this great and holy One will say when he appears? Yes. 'Would he contend with me

in the greatness of his power? No; he would pay attention to me ('put strength in me,' KJV, verse 6). God will not plead with me by his dread and terror and severity but will put strength in me.' Therefore, God bids them 'lay hold of my protection' (Isa. 27:5). Who dares to lay hold on God's arm? 'Let them lay hold of my protection, let them make peace with me, let them make peace with me.' Poor creatures are afraid to go to God because of his power, but 'fury is not in me,' says God.

(3) It is impossible for faith to consider God's nature without secretly viewing it in relationship to Jesus Christ, the daysman or arbiter between God and the soul; in relationship to him by whom God's severity and justice (and everything concerned with these properties of his nature) are already manifested and glorified.

(c) The third reason why the soul in overwhelming distresses will turn to God's nature, as revealed by his name, is taken from the nature of faith itself. The formal reason of faith is the truthfulness of God's word. What we believe with divine faith, we believe for this reason: that God has revealed and spoken it. And the ultimate object of faith is God's all-sufficiency. Whatever it is you may be directly exercising your faith upon, it will not rest and be satisfied until it comes, as it were, to be immersed in the all-sufficiency of God; like a stream of a river that runs with great speed and presses on until it comes to the ocean, where it is swallowed up. It is said, 'through Christ we are believers in God' (1 Pet. 1:21). Christ is the immediate object of faith, but God in his all-sufficiency is the ultimate object of faith.

Faith also acts in this way because it is the great principle of that divine nature that God has inlaid in our souls, which he has created within us, and of which he is the Father. 'Of his own will he brought us forth by the word of truth' (James 1:18). Faith, therefore, as it is the child of God – the new nature that God has engrafted within us – has a natural tendency towards God. It works in and through all towards God himself, who is its Father. This is the first thing that the soul considers in God; the first thing that faith applies to for relief.

2. *In overwhelming circumstances faith also finds relief in sovereign grace; that is, grace bestowed absolutely freely.*

What I mean by this is that which was mentioned previously, 'I will be gracious to whom I will be gracious, and will show mercy on whom I will show mercy' (Exod. 33:19). The things of which we stand in need are grace and mercy, and the principle from which they flow and are bestowed is the sovereign will and pleasure of God. God refers the dispensation of all grace and mercy to his own sovereign will and pleasure. When the soul can find nothing in the promise, nothing in any evidence of the love of God, or in any previous experience, it takes itself to the sovereignty of grace. It finds there two things:

(i) God is able to give relief in whatever state we find ourselves. Whatever is our need – mercy, life, salvation – God is able to give it. Whatever he wishes to do, he can do. Often in Scripture this is presented to us as an encouragement to rest upon God. When Shadrach, Meshach and Abednego were in that great, overwhelming danger, how did they comfort themselves? 'If this be so, our God whom we serve is able to deliver us from the burning fiery furnace, and he will deliver us out of your hand, O king. But if not, be it known to you, O king, that we will not serve your gods, or worship the golden image that you have set up' (Dan. 3:17). Notice, 'If God will not.' Not 'If God cannot,' for he can do whatever he wills. If he had not been able, they would not have worshipped him.

There is nothing in these last sixteen hundred years that seems harder to fulfil than the calling of the Jews. But the apostles provide this basis for our hopes as we wait for it: They 'will be grafted in, for God has the power to graft them in again' (Rom. 11:23). The very power of God – that he is able to do whatever he pleases – is a foundation for faith to act upon and find relief in so doing. God therefore pleads it strongly: 'Is my hand shortened, that it cannot redeem? Or have I no power to deliver? Behold, by my rebuke I dry up the sea, I make the rivers a desert ... I clothe the heavens with blackness and make sackcloth their covering' (Isa. 50:2, 3).

There are four things that are included in this apprehension of faith that God is able to do this, whatever our condition might be:

(1) There is nothing contrary to his own nature in it. There are things that are contrary to God's nature and these things God cannot do. 'God cannot lie' (Titus 1:2; Heb. 6:18). It is a part of God's infinite perfection that he can do nothing contrary to his own nature. Therefore, whatever I believe is of God's sovereign grace and is something he is able to do, I believe cannot include anything that is contrary to God's nature. Whatever apprehensions we have of pardon

of sin, it must include an atonement; for without an atonement God is not able to pardon our sins. God cannot do it without satisfaction to his justice. Therefore, every soul who apprehends that there is sovereign grace in God, by which he is able to relieve and help him, must include in that apprehension a belief in an atonement, without which God cannot do it. 'He cannot deny himself.' It is God's judgment 'that those who practise such things deserve to die' (Rom. 1:32).

(2) If God is able, there is nothing in it contrary to any decree of God. There are many things that may be contrary to God's decree which, in themselves, are not contrary to his nature; for the decree of God is a free act of his will, which might have been, or might not have been. But once the decree of God is engaged, if anything is contrary to it, God cannot do it, for God is not changeable.

The decree of God may be understood in two ways:

Firstly, his eternal purposes with respect to this or that person or thing. I am not referring to this.

Secondly, the decree of God involves *sententia lata*, a sentence that has already been determined, that God has pronounced against any person or thing. God will not proceed contrary to this. So, we are invited to seek the Lord 'before the decree takes effect' (Zeph. 2:2); that is, before the Lord has passed an absolute and determinate sentence in that matter or case. When Daniel would assure Nebuchadnezzar of his doom, he tells him it was 'a decree of the Most High' (Dan. 4:24). Saul's case is similar: 'The Lord has rejected you,' said Samuel (1 Sam. 15:26). But might he retract his sentence? No; 'The Glory of Israel will not lie' (verse 29). The sentence has gone forth, and it will stand. Similarly, God rejected the house of Eli from the priesthood (1 Sam. 2). But might he not change his mind? No; 'The iniquity of Eli's house shall not be atoned for by sacrifice or offering for ever' (1 Sam. 3:14). It was the same for those of whom God 'swore in his wrath, "They shall not enter my rest"' (Psa. 95:11; Heb. 3:11). While there is faith in God's sovereignty, if there is no decree involved in the case, there is hope. But if God had decreed and published his oath, he would not have raised my faith to look to his sovereign grace; this declares the ability in God, that he can do it.

(3) This faith in God's ability to grant us relief includes the following: that there is nothing in it contrary to the glory of God. This is the measure of everything that God does in all his dealings with us. He aims in all things at the manifestation of his glory. And we are not to desire anything that is contrary to the glory of God. We are not to desire that God would, for our sakes, fail to be holy and righteous, that we might be saved in our sins while still remaining obstinately in them. This is to desire that God might not be God, in order that we might live. But now, to save a humble, broken, contrite sinner – a poor guilty creature, who lies at his feet for mercy; to deliver poor distressed believers from ruin and oppression – is not inconsistent with the glory of God. God can do this for the advancement of his glory. I have known it be of great comfort to some poor souls when they could bring themselves to believe this, that to save and pardon them was not contrary to God's nature, decree and glory.

(4) There is this in it also: namely, that if there is need of power, God can provide it. That power carried Abraham

through all his difficulties: 'Is anything too hard for the Lord?' (Gen. 18:14). What is your distress? A wicked prevailing corruption? 'Is anything too hard for the Lord?' When external pressures weigh upon the church of God, there is relief in sovereign grace: 'Is anything too hard for the Lord?' Everything is too hard for us; but nothing is too hard for God. This is the first thing in sovereign grace: that God is able.

(ii) This being the case, all that we have to do is to commit everything to the will of God.

All I have to do in this world is only to go to God, as the leper did to Jesus. 'Lord, if you will, you can make me clean' (Matt. 8:2). If God wills it, he can pardon, sanctify, save me. And if God wills, he can deliver his church and his people. Here lies the whole question: it is all committed to his will.

If a poor soul has resolved all his concerns to the will of God, two things happen:

(a) All other entangling disputes and dark thoughts which overwhelm the mind will come to an end. 'For now,' says the soul, 'it has come to this, that my whole condition depends on God's sovereign pleasure.' David once complained that he was in the mire. A poor creature is sunk in the mud; the more he struggles, the faster he sticks. When a soul is in this condition, God tells him, 'Be still, and know that I am God' (Psa. 46:10). Everything is now dependent on the will of God.

(b) Once we are able to commit our situation absolutely, without further dispute, to the will of God, innumerable arguments will spring up to persuade the soul that God is willing. I will list some of them.

(1) One is taken from that goodness and graciousness of God's nature which we have already been considering, and which now arises in its proper place. Imagine that we had to deal with a man whom we believed to be a good man – a man who had something of God's image upon him – and the matter was to us of great importance (as much, perhaps, as our life was worth). And imagine that he could resolve the affair, without any prejudice or disadvantage to himself, by just one word. Could we cast any greater reflection upon this man than to think that he would be unwilling to act for us? That merely to do us mischief and out of spite, he would change his own nature and act against his own principles? Shall we, then, question the goodwill of God? Shall we fear that with everything dependent on his will, he will not act with grace and mercy in time of need? Our Saviour presses home this argument (Luke 11:11-13 and other places), applying it almost directly to our present context; telling us that it is not to be expected that a child would not trust his father to give him bread, if this depended solely on the father's goodwill. 'If you then, who are evil, know how to give good gifts to your children, how much more will the heavenly Father give the Holy Spirit to those who ask him!' When we can present the concerns of God's church and his people to his mere will, his own nature will supply us with enough arguments to confirm our hope that he will act.

(2) There is another great argument, when all is brought to the sovereignty of God's will, found in Romans 8:32. 'He who did not spare his own Son but gave him up for us all, how will he not also with him graciously give us all things?' Shall I question whether or not God will answer this prayer or the other, when I consider this great example of his will?

It was his will to send Jesus Christ to die for poor sinners. He did not send him to die in vain, and that his death should be lost. If God is not willing to dispense grace and mercy to sinners, why did he send Jesus Christ? Why did he give up his own Son out of his bosom? Why did he not spare him and leave our iniquities to meet upon us? Can God give a greater sign of his readiness to spare sinners than the way in which he dealt with Jesus Christ? This is the second thing which faith considers when it comes to God for relief in an overwhelming condition: sovereign grace; that God is able, and that all things are committed to his will.

(3) Faith, in this context, takes account of that one particular property of God's grace mentioned in Ephesians 3:8: 'the unsearchable riches of Christ.' Faith responds, 'There is more grace and more mercy too in God (for it is God's riches that are referred to here) than I can possibly see or consider. Will the mercy that has been declared to my faith, the promises that have been revealed and discovered to me, satisfy me? No, they will not. I cannot be satisfied with what I have received, with the discoveries made to me of the grace of God.' 'But,' says the soul, 'beyond what I have received, lie unsearchable riches of grace, of which I have no conception, which all the world, or all the angels in heaven, cannot find out.' This is a great relief to an over-burdened soul.

(4) Again, faith in such a condition learns how to understand former experiences, not in terms of its present experience, but in terms of the unchangeableness of God. If this is done wisely, it is sufficient to relieve our souls when in many overwhelming distresses. The psalmist shows this in Psalm 77. He had known an experience of God: 'Let me

remember my song in the night' (verse 6). Compare this with Job's experience: 'Where is God my Maker, who gives songs in the night?' (Job 35:10). David is referring to some experience, one night, of the love and goodwill of God that made him rejoice. But what is his situation at present? He tells us (verse 2) that it is 'the day of my trouble'; that his 'sore ran in the night and ceased not' (KJV); his 'soul refused to be comforted.' He continues, 'Will the Lord spurn for ever, and never again be favourable? Has his steadfast love for ever ceased? Has God forgotten to be gracious? Has he in anger shut up his compassion?' (verses 7-9). In this great and overwhelming trouble where does he find relief? He commits his experience to the unchangeableness of God: 'This is my infirmity; but I will remember the years of the right hand of the most High' (verse 10, KJV). 'Though now I have nothing but darkness and am ready to fear that his mercy has been removed for ever, yet he who gave me that former song in the night season, he is ever the same, and he will give similar experiences again. Though I am changed, he is not.'

3. *I should go further, and show what respect faith has, in such a condition, to the covenant of God.* But I have no time now to consider this.

4. *I had also intended, lastly, to describe the difference between the faith of the godly and that of unbelievers.*

That faith which the worst of men will have in God when they are in trouble, compared to the relief which true evangelical faith finds in an overwhelming condition. But I see that this also would take up too much time.

Application

One word of application, and then I will finish.

The present is an overwhelming time; a time when many are at the ends of the earth literally, and many metaphorically. A time and a season in which most who fear the Lord suffer some distress or other. Suppose that it were the case that God had not, in these days, poured out upon many an overwhelming sense of guilt; that there were not many tempted, wounded and troubled (though there are some, whom we meet with every day). Yet, I have great reason to fear that if we were all rightly convicted, an overwhelming distress would fall upon us all, because of our lack of humility, holiness, fruitfulness, faith and love. We once enjoyed such virtues, they are still held up before us, and the examples of those who have gone before us encourage us to seek them. Are none overwhelmed with hardness of heart, instability of spirit? Overgrown with careless, empty, light, worldly frames? Truly, we all, to some degree or other, have reason to be overwhelmed, and I have shown you a little of where we may find relief in this state and condition.

Are we ready to be overwhelmed by the calamitous condition of the people of God all over the world, and of ourselves, our goods and personal concerns, everything that is near and dear to us? I pray that God will make our hearts jealous over it, especially those that are at ease in their health and prosperity. When God throws others of his people into the furnace, these have great reason to be jealous, in case he deals more severely with them than the poorest saint in want of a morsel of bread. Well, I have shown you the way of relief in this case also. It is to God alone that we must apply. He is willing to receive us because of the goodness of his nature, and he is able to save us because of the abundance of his grace and power.

Sermon 11

The Christian's Work of Dying Daily[1]

*'I protest by your rejoicing which I have in Christ Jesus our
Lord, I die daily.*—1 Cor. 15:31, KJV

THESE words express a great vehemence and emphasis,
revealing a considerable urgency in the apostle's spirit as he
wrote them. In the original they carry an even greater sense
of import than in our translation. 'I die daily' comes first
in the original. Then follows, 'Yes, I do so by your rejoicing
which I have in Christ Jesus our Lord.' There is no other
expression used by the apostle that has a greater ardour of
spirit than this.

The special reason for using it in this place is to testify
to the stability of his faith with regard to the resurrection
of the dead. You know that this is the issue with which he
is dealing. He proves here that he was not expressing an
opinion but a firm-rooted faith that carried him through
all difficulties and sufferings. 'Why am I in danger every
hour? I protest, brothers, by my pride in you, which I have
in Christ Jesus our Lord, I die every day! What do I gain if,
humanly speaking, I fought with beasts at Ephesus? If the

[1] Preached on 26 September, 1680

dead are not raised, "Let us eat and drink, for tomorrow we die"' (ESV). 'I testify to my faith in the resurrection,' he says, 'by my readiness to suffer all things in order to confirm its truth.' It is the great duty of ministers to be ready at all times to testify to the strength of their own faith in the things which they preach to others, by a cheerful suffering because of them.

There are two things in these words: an assertion, and the confirmation of that assertion. The assertion is this: 'I die daily.' The confirmation: 'I protest by your rejoicing which I have in Christ Jesus our Lord.'

There are also two difficulties with the words. I will not trouble you much with the different conjectures but give what I think is the sense of the Holy Spirit in them.

The first is from the ambiguous meaning of the word which is translated here (in the KJV) 'rejoicing.' But in other places it is rendered 'confidence,' 'boasting,' or 'glorying' (or 'pride,' ESV). 'Gloriation' is the word I would use, if there were such a word in our language. 'By my gloriation'; an expression of exultant joy.

There is another difficulty in the transposition of the words, which are not found elsewhere in the Scriptures: 'I protest by your rejoicing which I have in Christ Jesus.' This has produced a variety of conjectures, but plainly the sense of it is, 'By the rejoicing which you and I have in the Lord.' I could give instances of similar transpositions in the Greek language, from one person to another, if it were to your benefit.

There is still a third difficulty. The particle used here denotes an oath, yet sometimes it is used as a note of strong emphasis. It is translated here by the medial expression,

'I protest.' If it is understood as expressing an oath, then the word denotes the object: 'I swear by your rejoicing in the Lord'; that is, 'by the Lord in whom you rejoice.' As we find in Genesis 31:53, 'Jacob swore by the Fear of his father Isaac'; that is, 'by him whom his father Isaac feared.' But I understand it here as a note of vehement affirmation: 'It is as true as that you and I glory in Christ and rejoice in him, that I die daily.'

The whole phrase may have a double sense. It could mean, 'Because I preach the gospel, I am every day exposed to death and danger.' For Paul often wrote, before and after this time, of the dangers he underwent in his work of preaching the gospel. Or it might mean, 'I die daily by the act of continually preparing myself to die. I am always preparing to die. Through faith in the resurrection, I am always prepared to die cheerfully and comfortably, according to the will of God.' I shall base my remarks on this second meaning and, consequently, find in this experience of the apostle a general rule for all.

Observation

It is the duty of all believers to be preparing themselves every day to die cheerfully, comfortably and, if it may be, triumphing in the Lord.

Take note of this: that one may die safely without dying cheerfully and comfortably. Every believer, whoever he or she is, shall die safely. But we see many believers who do not die cheerfully and comfortably. I am not going to refer to the first truth – how all believers die safely – but to the second: how believers may die cheerfully and comfortably.

There are two ways of dying cheerfully and comfortably:

1. The first is in our external aspect, to the comfort of those who are around us. This depends a great deal on the nature of the disease of which men die, which may bring with it a depression of spirit and clouding of the mind. This aspect is not under our control but must be left to God's providence.

2. But there is also a cheerful and comfortable death experienced in a person's soul, which, perhaps, in their dying moments, they may not be able to testify to, though being fully prepared for it.

Truly, brothers and sisters, all I can say is that I have thought much about these things for my own account, before I ever thought of presenting them to you. I will not tell you how far I have proceeded in this matter, which may be little or nothing, but only what I have aimed at, in the hope that this might be of use to us in this dying time. This seems to be especially true in the case of godly ministers, one or another dying every day.[2]

---

[2] At this time many eminent servants of Christ, who had been associated with Owen in the Christian ministry and in important public duties during the eventful times of the Protectorate, were passing into their eternal rest. In 1679, Thomas Goodwin, President of Magdalene College, a member of the Westminster Assembly, a happy expositor of Scripture, and, according to Anthony Wood, 'one of the Atlases and Patriarchs of Independency,' was removed from this world, and became, in the highest sense of his own phrase, 'a child of light.' It was but two months before this sermon was preached that Stephen Charnock died. He had been a Senior Proctor in the University of Oxford during the Protectorate and

I shall mention three things that, in my judgment, are necessary for every believer wishing to die cheerfully and to come, in the full and proper time, into the presence of God.

I. *The constant exercise of faith with respect to the resigning of a departing soul into the hand and sovereign will of God.*

'I die daily.' How? Exercising faith constantly in the resigning of a departing soul, when the time comes, to the sovereign grace, good pleasure, power and faithfulness of God. The soul is now taking its leave of all its concerns in this world; all that it sees, all that it knows by its senses, all its relationships, everything with which it has been acquainted up till now. From now on it will be absolutely, eternally unconcerned with them. It is entering into an invisible world of which it knows nothing, except what it has by faith. When Paul was taken up into the third heaven (2 Cor. 12:2-4) we would have been glad to have heard some description from the invisible world of how things were there. He saw nothing; he only heard words. May we not hear those words, blessed Paul? No. 'They cannot be told.' God does not wish us to know anything about the

---

had left behind him manuscripts from which two large folios of posthumous works have been published; works held in such estimation that, besides the detached issue of particular treatises, they have been, in their collected form, four times reprinted. Others might be mentioned who died about this period, such as Matthew Poole, author of the 'Synopsis Criticorum'; and Theophilus Gale, author of 'The Court of the Gentiles.' Such facts may help to account for the touching and solemn tone of these discourses on preparation for death, as well as for the particular allusion in the paragraph above.—W. H. Goold.

invisible world while we are here, except what is revealed in the word. Therefore, I am sure that the souls of those who have departed – who have died, but then lived again, such as the soul of Lazarus – were supported in their being by God, but that he restrained all their operation. For if a departed soul had one natural immediate view of God it would be the greatest misery in the world to be sent back into a dying body. God keeps those things to be the objects of faith. Lazarus could tell nothing of what was done in heaven; his soul was kept in existence, but all its operations were restrained. I bless God I have exercised my thoughts regarding the invisible world only on what is revealed in the word. Of this, perhaps, in due time, you may hear something; but in the meantime, I know that we have no notion of it except from pure revelation.

Where now is my soul going? What will be the end in a short while? Will it be annihilated? Does death not only separate the body and soul but also destroy our being, so that to all eternity we will be no more? That is how some will have it; it is in their interest that it should be so. Or is the soul passing into a state of wandering in the air, under the influence of more powerful spirits? That was the opinion of the old pagan world, who understood it as the reason for the frequent appearances of the dead upon earth.

And this pagan belief was developed by the Papists into the idea of purgatory, from which they concluded that there were continual appearances on earth of those who had departed. There followed therefore a thousand stories of such appearances, which we all know to be the actions and deceits of evil spirits. And such is our darkness with regard to the invisible world that the majority of Christians have invented this third state of purgatory; one which is entirely the fruit of superstition and idolatry. This is indeed the nature of superstition: the inventing of things in religion which are suited to men's natural feelings, or to the gratification of their lusts for their own profit. Both motives were at work in this case. For, when people thought that the souls of those who had passed into an eternal state were for ever lost, 'No,' they said, 'there is another chance for them.' And so they reassured themselves that, even if they were the worst of men, yet there might be hope for them after death. The belief does not in any way decrease any tendency in them to gratify their lusts or dissuade them from living at their pleasure. All this its devisors turned to their own profit. This is mentioned in passing only as one example of the darkness which mankind is in with respect to the invisible world.

But does the soul go to a state in which it is incapable of joy or consolation? Brothers and sisters, let men pretend what they will, those who never received any joy or comfort in this world except by their senses, or by their reason being exercised about the objects of sense, do not know, or can ever believe, that the soul itself is capable of consolation in another world. Only someone who has received spiritual comfort immediately into his soul in this world can believe that his soul is capable of it in another. But still, this is certain: no man can be assured of anything about the life of the soul in another world.

What is your path forward, then, in this state and condition? What is the wise approach? Truly, to resign this departing soul to the sovereign wisdom, pleasure, faithfulness and power of God (the duty under consideration) by the continual exercise of faith. The apostle tells us, 'I know whom I have believed, and I am convinced that he is able to guard until that Day what has been entrusted to me' (2 Tim. 1:12). It is a mighty thing to keep an individual soul until the day of resurrection. 'I know to whom I have trusted it,' says Paul. 'I have trusted it to almighty power.' May the Lord help us to believe that there will be an act of almighty power put forth on behalf of our poor souls when departed into the invisible world, to keep them until that day when body and soul shall be united and proceed to enjoy God.

We have a glorious example of this duty and exercise of faith. Our Lord Jesus Christ died in the exercise of it. It was the last act of faith that Christ demonstrated in this world: 'Then Jesus, calling out with a loud voice (that was the voice of nature), said (he now comes to the words of faith), "Father, into your hands I commit my spirit (my departing soul)." And having said this he breathed his last' (Luke 23:46). This was the last exercise of the faith of our Lord Jesus Christ in this world: the committing of his departing soul into the hands of God. And for what purpose did he do it? We are told in Psalm 16:8-11:

> I have set the Lord always before me; because he is at my right hand, I shall not be shaken.
> Therefore my heart is glad, and my whole being rejoices; my flesh also dwells secure.
> For you will not abandon my soul to Sheol, or let your holy one see corruption.
> You make known to me the path of life; in your presence there is fullness of joy; at your right hand are pleasures for evermore.

These are the words of David, which our Lord Jesus Christ applied to himself when he said, 'Into your hands I commit my spirit,' and the psalmist adds, 'You have redeemed me, O Lord, faithful God' (Psa. 31:5). An experience of the work of redemption communicated to us by the truth of the promise is the greatest encouragement to commend a departing soul into God's hands.

When we consider the vanishing of all these shadows and appearances and the eternal dissolution of all relationships with things here below, and the existence of the soul in a separate condition with which we are quite unfamiliar, here is one of the first things to consider if we are to die cheerfully and comfortably: how we must resign a departing soul into the hand and sovereign disposal of God.

It is both a great and eminent act of faith and also the last, victorious, act of faith:

1. *It is a great and eminent act of faith.*

The great efficacy and success of faith is spoken of in Hebrews 11. The phrase 'These all died in faith' is central for many of those mentioned in the chapter. It was a great thing to die in faith under the Old Testament, when they were surrounded by so many shadows and so much darkness, and when their view of invisible things, within the veil, was so much less than that which God has shown us. In fact, the state of things within the veil was not the same then as it is now. Christ was not then upon the throne, administering his office. Yet, faith carried them through all this darkness and caused them to trust their souls to God, to his faithfulness, mercy and grace.

To think of these things is to lay all things in the balance. In the one scale: our being, our walk and life in this world; our sins and their guilt; our fears, uncertainties and the darkness of a future state; our abhorrence of a dissolution, and the thought of everything around us. In the other scale: the power, faithfulness and mercy of God, and his ability to receive, preserve and keep us to that day, and to be more to us than all earthly things. 'This will be my choice,' says faith. 'Everything in the first scale is of no value, no weight, compared to the exceeding weight of the power and goodness of God.' This is a glorious exercise of faith. Have you tried it, brothers and sisters? Lay things on one side or the other in a balance and see which way the scale will fall, what faith will do in your case.

2. *It is the last victorious act of faith, in which it has its final conquest over all its adversaries.*

Faith is the leading grace in all our spiritual warfare and conflict, but throughout life it has faithful company that adhere to it and help it. Love works, and hope works, and all the other graces – self-denial, readiness for the cross – they all work and help faith. But when we come to die, faith is left alone. Now faith is tested. The exercise of the other graces ceases. Only faith comes to this close conflict with the last adversary, in which the whole is to be tried. And, by this one act of resigning all into the hands of God, faith triumphs over death and cries, '"O death, where is your victory? O death, where is your sting?" Come, give me an entry into immortality and glory; the everlasting hand of God is ready to receive me!' This is the victory by which we overcome all our spiritual enemies.

I had thought of making use of what I have said, of examining whether we do live in the exercise of this grace or not, and of what benefit we receive from doing so. And I would have mentioned one particular benefit, namely, that it will keep us from all surprise at death. Not to be surprised by anything in this life is the core of human wisdom; not to be surprised at death is a major part of the core of spiritual wisdom.

Sermon 12

The Christian's Work of
Dying Daily (*Cont.*)

'I protest by your rejoicing which I have in Christ Jesus our
Lord, I die daily.—1 Cor. 15:31, KJV

I BEGAN to expound this portion of Scripture last Lord's
Day and I thought the subject would be very suitable for us
because of the warning given to us by God in various ways
that we should be exercising ourselves in this duty. Since
that day,[1] God has increased the timeliness of the message
by taking away a great and eminent servant of his from
among us.[2] I will say just one word with respect to him:

[1] Preached on 3 October, 1680.
[2] The decease to which Owen refers must have occurred between
September 26 and October 3. Colonel Desborough, a member of
his congregation, brother-in-law to Oliver Cromwell, and one of
the heroes of the Commonwealth, died on 10 September 1680.
He refused to sit on the trial of Charles I; and though so nearly
related to Cromwell, opposed him when he sought to become
king. But it is evident, from the dates, that the allusion cannot
be to him. The quaint and pious Thomas Brooks, a preacher of
distinguished pathos and usefulness, and author of some well-
known treatises, such as *Heaven upon Earth*, *The Unsearchable*

As far as I can judge, by thirty years' acquaintance and friendship, and half that time in church-fellowship, it may be that the age in which he lived did not produce many more wise, more holy, more useful than he in his station, if any. And so, I leave him at rest with God.

I propose to discuss those things which are necessary for us to obtain a peaceful and comfortable departure out of this world. I have mentioned one point; namely, the daily exercise of faith, in the resignation of a departing soul to the sovereign power and will of God, to be treated and received by him according to the tenor of the covenant of God.

I will not leave this point without applying it, limiting my time only by the strength God gives me.

Application 1

It may be worth our while to look at the particular nature of this duty to which we are called, for each passing day shows us the weakness of many who think that, perhaps, they know something of it, but in fact have no knowledge at all of what is involved. We will consider three things:

(i) What is the specific and immediate object of this exercise of faith;

(ii) What is its form or nature; and

(iii) How is it carried out and fulfilled.

Riches of Christ, Apples of Gold in Pictures of Silver, etc., died on 27 September, 1680. The date would answer to the allusion in the discourse, if the terms of it did not leave an impression that Owen refers to a member of his own congregation. Brooks was a zealous Congregationalist; but this could hardly be all the 'church-fellowship' to which Owen refers. In his work, *The Golden Key*, he subscribes himself 'late preacher of the word at Margaret's, New Fish Street.'—W. H. Goold.

(i) The specific and immediate object of this exercise of faith, arising from a specific motive, is God, viewed with respect to his sovereignty, power and faithfulness, and motivated by some experience of his kindness and grace.

The psalmist notes, 'Into your hand I commit my spirit' (Psa. 31:5). What was it that gave him confidence to do so? 'You have redeemed me,' he says, 'O Lord, faithful God.' A sense of redeeming grace, conveyed by the truth of the promises, is needed by all who would commit their souls into the hand of God. Therefore, brothers and sisters, when you come to fulfil this great duty, you must base it upon some sense and experience that you have of the grace and kindness of God; otherwise you will not fulfil it appropriately.

(a) With this motive, the first thing to consider, in resigning our souls to him, is God's sovereignty. This is mentioned in two places in the Psalms, in both of which this duty is being referred to. 'Preserve me, O God, for in you I take refuge. I say to the Lord (that is, 'to *Jehovah*'), "You are my God"' (Psa. 16:1, 2). He does not use the Hebrew word for *Jehovah* again, but that for 'Lord, Master' (*Adonai*). 'You are my Master, who has the sovereign disposal over me. I am going to give up my spirit to you, and I do so on consideration of your sovereignty, that "you are my Master."' We find the same in Psa. 31:14, 15: 'But I trust in you, O Lord.' Why can he say this? 'I say, "You are my God. My times are in your hand."' 'It is because of your sovereignty. "You are my God" who has sovereign disposal over me, therefore I commit myself to you.' This thought follows the words, 'Father, into your hand I commit my spirit' (verse 5). Faith, when it resigns the soul to God, looks at the glorious sovereignty of God as the absolute free disposer of all things here and for eternity, with no restraint upon him other than his own pleasure.

(b) Faith also looks particularly at the power of God. 'I know whom I have believed, and I am convinced that he is able to guard until that Day what has been entrusted to me' (2 Tim. 1:12). It is usual for people to pass through death as a matter of needs must. Die they must. Nothing can encourage them to yield up their souls to God other than an apprehension of such an infinite power that is able to preserve them in eternal being in the invisible world, until the day of resurrection.

(c) Faith looks to God in his faithfulness, as one who has promised that he will take care of us when we leave this world. 'Therefore, let those who suffer according to God's will entrust their souls to a faithful Creator while doing good' (1 Pet. 4:19); that is, to a God who is omnipotent, who made all things and is faithful in accomplishing all his promises.

This duty, then, to which I am exhorting you, is a direct address to God, an exercise of faith upon him, with particular regard to his sovereignty, power and faithfulness, and based on the experience we have, to some degree, of his goodness and grace.

The seat in front of me has changed in a very short time, and I do not know, brothers and sisters, how soon any of you will stand in need of an understanding of this duty, and of fulfilling it. Remember it, if you please, because it is so important to have direct dealings with God with respect to these great and awful attributes of his sovereignty, power and faithfulness. This is the first point.

(ii) As to the nature of this duty, there are two words by which it is expressed, both having the same significance. In one reference it is rendered 'commending,' and in another, 'committing' (Luke 23:46, KJV, and Psa. 31:5, respectively). In both cases it is an act of recommending or committing, just as when men commit a trust. If a man were to be dying and had an only child, or an estate, to leave behind, with what solemnity would he commit them to the trust of his friend to care for them! 'I commit this poor child, who is helpless and fatherless; I commit him to your trust,' he says, 'to your love, care and power; to look after him.' He would do it with great solemnity. The psalmist calls his soul his 'precious life' and his 'only one' (Psa. 22:20; 35:17): 'Deliver my precious life from the power of the dog.' When a person is about to leave this world he has to commit his soul and leave it in trust somewhere. This exercise of faith is then the leaving in trust, or committing, our 'precious one' that is departing from this tabernacle to God, with due regard to his sovereignty, power and faithfulness. And the heart of this duty, the solemnity of the committal, consists in commending the care of our souls to God to be dealt with, not according to our choice, but according to the terms of the covenant of grace, be that what it may, to all eternity.

(iii) As to how this duty is carried out, it ought to be done in words expressed directly to God. I am not instructing those who are dying, but you who live, in order that you should be prepared to die. You should say to God, 'Lord, I have been this long in the world; I have seen much variety in the outward disposal of things, but a thousand times more variety in the inward frame of my spirit. I am now leaving the world at your call. I am to be no more. O Lord, all being over, being about to enter a new, eternal state, I commit my soul to you – I leave it with you – I put all my trust and confidence in your faithfulness, power and sovereignty, to be dealt with according to the terms of the covenant of grace. Now I can lie down in peace.'

Application 2

What benefit will we receive if we do exercise our faith in this way? We will receive the following advantages:

(i) Nothing will keep our souls in more constant reverence towards God, which is the very life and soul of our holiness and obedience. Where this is absent, the greatest profession of faith is of no value. There is nothing better for us than a direct approach to God every day (and frequently every day) to consider his glorious sovereignty, power and faithfulness, as if you were about to be entering his presence and being committed into his hands. The more you abound in it, the greater will your reverence of God be. We have deceitful hearts and a very skilful adversary to deal with. We are commanded to draw near and to approach God with boldness: 'With confidence draw near to the throne of God' (Heb. 4:16; 10:19). And we should do it frequently. But nothing in this world is so suited to undermine reverence than confidence and frequency. Where men are confident and frequent – as in so many duties they are – it diminishes reverence to God. I am referring to *carnal* confidence. But the more frequently you approach God in *spiritual* confidence, the more will your hearts be filled continually with reverence towards him. Conversely, the more frequently you approach God in outward duties without this holy and humble reverence, no matter what your gifts might be, the more reverence towards God will decay. What poor, slight, shrivelled things have I seen men grow to be, with an acceptable outward conversation, and a multiplicity of duties! And you can take this gauge with you in all your duties: if they increase within you a reverence for God, they are from grace; if they do not, they are from gifts, and do not sanctify those who possess them in any way.

(ii) It will support us in all our sufferings. The soul that is accustomed to this exercise of faith will not be greatly disturbed in all its troubles. The Lord knows we are all moved and shaken – and ready to be so, sometimes roughly and excessively – like the leaves of a forest. But this will keep us from being greatly moved. 'I shall not be greatly shaken,' says the psalmist (Psa. 62:2), and, as already mentioned, we are told, 'let those who suffer according to God's will entrust their souls to a faithful Creator.' This will support you under all your sufferings. It is exactly the situation found in Psalm 31, from which I have taken the text we have been considering: 'Be gracious to me, O Lord, for I am in distress; my eye is wasted from grief; my soul and my body also. For my life is spent with sorrow, and my years with sighing; my strength fails because of my iniquity, and my bones waste away, etc.' (verses 9, 10); 'For I hear the whispering of many – terror on every side! – as they scheme together against me, as they plot to take my life' (verse 13). What course does he then take in all these distresses, suffering and persecution? 'I say, "You are my God." My times are in your hand.' He resigned himself to the sovereignty of God, and so was at peace.

I have therefore now shown you how to exercise this duty. I judge that my own account is near at hand and speak to you as someone who is aware of this. I wish that I could prevail upon you to fulfil this duty before you give your eyes to sleep this night!

Application 3

In the next place, who are those who are able to fulfil this duty, who live in the exercise of this faith?

I am certain that those who live as if their life on earth was to last forever, do not do so. This is a clear proof of that disease and confusion which has fallen upon the mind and soul of man. If a man of sobriety and reputation ever came upon such men, of which the world is full, living in their sensuality and wickedness, and told them, 'Sirs, what are you doing? I am persuaded that there is a death to come, and an eternal state of blessedness or woe approaching. Your way of life will certainly engulf you in eternal destruction'; they would say to him, 'That is your opinion.' Yet you would think that the words of the wise man would prevail upon them to respond in some way to his belief. But this is not so. They are convicted in their minds that they must die. They will not merely say that this is my opinion or yours; they are convinced themselves that there is a future state and will profess that belief. But will they do anything in response to this conviction? Nothing at all; no more than if they were brute animals. They are not able to approach the exercise of this duty.

Nor are those who walk carelessly, by chance. They know they must die, but they tend to think that they have other things to do before they die, and that there will be time enough, at some later season or other, to prepare to die. The apostle, indeed, did 'die daily,' but these have something else to do. When death knocks at their neighbour's door and they hear that such and such a person is dead, or when it comes to their own families and takes away this or that person, then they have some thoughts for a little while. But these quickly wear off, and they return to their usual frame again. '"A little sleep, a little slumber, a little folding of the hands to rest" (Prov. 6:10-12); a little more secure converse in the world, attending to our affairs.' But death will come as an armed man and they will not be able to escape.

There are, therefore, two things needed by everyone who wishes to be found fulfilling this duty:

(i) That he lays the foundation of it on a clear persuasion of an interest in Christ.

This alone will ensure that he will die in safety. Having obtained this, he may labour for that which will enable him to die comfortably and cheerfully. Some men die safely but, for many reasons, which we will not go into now, they do not appear to die comfortably. And some men die very comfortably, to all outward appearance, who do not die safely. This, therefore, is necessary, that this foundation should be laid: a sure persuasion of our interest in Christ, that we may die safely. Otherwise, there is no point in expecting to die comfortably.

(ii) That he has a view of eternal things.

Many think that a few words at the last will do it, ensuring a happy end, but let me assure you, not only on principles of scriptural truth but on those of nature, that no man who does not have a view of the glory of spiritual and eternal things that is of greater weight than all that his soul finds in this world, can do it. No man under heaven can part with that which appears good to him, unless he is motivated by a greater good. He must part with it, but he cannot do so willingly and cheerfully. If you wish to part willingly and cheerfully with your soul, resigning it to God, labour to have a clear view of these better things – which are infinitely greater and more glorious – into the enjoyment of which your souls will enter at the moment of their departure.

The calls of God upon us, both public and private, are great, especially upon this congregation. God requires a particular obedience from us; otherwise we can expect to be exercised with further tokens of his displeasure.

Sermon 13

The Christian's Work of Dying Daily (*Cont.*)[1]

'I protest by your rejoicing which I have in Christ Jesus our Lord, I die daily.—1 Cor. 15:31, KJV

WHAT I have been expounding from these words are the ways and duties by which a believer may come to die, not only safely, which all believers shall, but cheerfully and comfortably, so as to have a free and abundant entrance into the kingdom of God in glory.

I have been speaking on one point only: the exercise of faith in the resigning of a departing soul entering the invisible world into the sovereign hand and pleasure of God, to be disposed of according to the tenor of the everlasting covenant.

There are still two things necessary in this exercise (at least, I find them so) that remain to be considered. These, God willing, we shall proceed to elaborate.

II. *To fulfil this great duty there must be a readiness and willingness to part with this body which we carry about with us and to lay it down in the dust.*

[1] Preached on 10 October, 1680.

The soul's natural aversion to let go of the body is what I mean by an unwillingness to die. It has made some say, like him of old, '*Mori nolo*, etc.' – 'I am happy to be dead, but I do not wish to die.'

There are two reasons why the soul is naturally unwilling to part with the body:

1. *Because it is, and has always been from the beginning, the only instrument of all the operations and actions of the soul's faculties and powers.*

The main freedom of a being lies in its powers and actions. From the first moment of its being, the soul has no instrument by which to act other than the body. Not only in the outward actions, but in all the internal, rational actions, the soul cannot act without the instrumentality of the body. This is why an injury to the body, particularly to the head, may deprive the soul completely from exercising all its powers and faculties. It requires the body to perform rational, internal actions, and it has no knowledge of how to act without a body. This has produced a natural unwillingness in the soul to let the body go.

The second reason is stronger still:

2. *It arises from the strict, close and unparalleled relationship and union between the body and the soul.*

There is a near union between parents and children, a nearer union still between husband and wife, but there is nothing to compare to this union between soul and body. There is an ineffable, inconceivable union between the two natures, the divine and the human, in the person of the Son of God, but this union was eternally indissoluble from its first existence. When the body and soul of Christ were separated, yet they continued in their individual unions with the person of the Son of God as much as before, or as now in heaven. But here is a union which is dissoluble, between a heavenly spirit and an earthly, sensual body; that is, two essential parts of the same nature. Allow me, please, to speak on this a little. I have mentioned what is involved in dying and noted the difficulty involved in our death. It arises, as I have said, from the constitution of our nature; there is nothing like it in all the works of God, in heaven above, or in the earth beneath. The angels are pure, immaterial spirits; they have nothing in them that can die. God can annihilate an angel – he that made all things out of nothing can bring all things to nothing – but the constitution of an angel cannot pass through death; there is nothing in him that can die. An animal has nothing in it that can live when life goes. Solomon says of 'the spirit of the beast' that it 'goes down into the earth' (Eccles. 3:21). It is not the purpose of almighty power to preserve it, because an animal consists only of the physical actions of its physical constitution. In contrast, man is '*medium participationis*'; he has an angelic nature from above that cannot die, and a nature from below that cannot live forever since the entrance of sin, though it might have done so before. Therefore, in bringing man into being there was a double act of creation, but only a single act in the creation of any other creature. The creation of angels is not mentioned (unless there is reference in the words, '"Let there be light," and there was light'), but in all other things there was only one single act for its production. But when God came to make man, there were two distinct acts of creation. 'The Lord God formed the man of dust from the ground.' And what then? 'And breathed into his nostrils the breath of life' (Gen. 2:7). Here is something not found elsewhere in all God's creation. And now, as this unity is dissolved, all the actions of this human nature, as found in one person, must end until the day of resurrection. This is a remarkable change: that there shall be no more united action of the entire nature of man until the resurrection; only one part of this nature continues to act according to its own powers.

One purpose of God's work upon us in the grave is to free our bodies from all alliance and relationships, and from all likeness to the bodies of animals. Our Saviour therefore tells us, 'Do not be mistaken. You shall neither marry nor be given in marriage,' nor have any relationships common to the animals; 'but the whole man shall be equal to angels' (Luke 20:34-36). This is the great privilege of our nature, as the wise man describes when he answers the following objection of an epicure: '"What happens to the children of man and what happens to beasts is the same; as one dies, so dies the other. They all have the same breath, and man has no advantage over the beasts, for all is vanity. All go to one place. All are from the dust, and to dust all return." As far as I can see, this is the case,' says the man. But what is the wise man's answer? 'Who knows whether the spirit of man goes upwards and the spirit of the beast goes down into the earth?' (Eccles. 3:19-21). 'Alas, you are mistaken,' says the wise man. 'The difference does not lie in this outward nature, in which man and beast are closely related to each other, but in the spiritual, heavenly nature, that is from above. And unless you know that, you will indeed think that we are just like the beasts.' This then is the basis of that unalterable aversion in the mind and soul to part with the body. This strange constitution of our nature that has nothing like it in the whole work of God, nothing to which we can compare it; it is unique to ourselves. Furthermore, this dissolution only happens once. They say of the heroes of old, who would freely risk their lives, and throw them away in some great venture, that when they came to die, when they had killed themselves or been killed by others, their souls departed with groaning and indignation. They did not know how to bear the dissolution of the union.

This is part of all of us, brothers and sisters. Our first desire, arising from any awareness of impending death, is 'that we would be further clothed,' as the apostle says, 'that what is mortal may be swallowed up by life' (2 Cor. 5:4); that the body and soul may go together into immortality and glory. But this is not God's way. What he aims for is to bring us to a state of readiness and willingness to part with these bodies of ours, notwithstanding the union. Without this, we cannot die cheerfully and comfortably.

Upon what grounds, then, can a man be ready and willing to lay down his tabernacle in the dust?

I shall mention two reasons, both given by the apostle Paul:

(i) The first is this: 'My desire is to depart and be with Christ' (Phil. 1:23). 'I have a strong bent and inclination of spirit.' The original Greek word is used in Scripture for 'lust' and 'covetousness'; that is, an inclination and desire that is always at work. 'It is not a desire that is sometimes present, now and then, when in trouble, sickness or pain, but I have a habitual, constant desire.' For what? 'To depart,' to leave this body. The original Greek word is usually translated in the passive: 'I have a desire to be dissolved.' But the plain meaning of the word is this: 'I desire that the substance of my nature may be reduced into its distinct parts, may be resolved.' Now, resolution of speech is the reducing of speech from the present form into its proper, distinct principles. So here, then, we have a difficulty. I have told you that the soul has a strong aversion to this dissolution, yet the apostle says, 'I have a continual strong inclination to it.' But for what reason? And notice his answer: 'To be with Christ.' I have no desire to be dissolved as an end in itself, but only as the means to another end. Without it I cannot be with Christ. That is my end. And with respect to that end, something which of itself I do not desire becomes an object of desire. Brothers and sisters, I know that no-one dies willingly – no living person can continually be desiring to meet cheerfully with death – except by looking at it as a means of coming to the enjoyment of Christ. Your bodies are more to you than all the world, all your possessions, or anything else, but Christ is better for the soul than anything. Therefore, unless it is for the enjoyment of Christ, whatever men may pretend, they will never be willing to part with their bodies, to be dissolved. But if that desire for coming to Christ grows within you, you will conquer the unwillingness for death.

(ii) The second reason is given in Romans 8:10, 'The body is dead because of sin, the Spirit is life because of righteousness.' The body is not only doomed to death because of original sin, in that death spread to all men because of sin, but the body must also be brought to death in order that sin might be rooted out of it. Sin has taken such a close, inseparable habitation in the body that nothing but the death of the body can separate them. The body must be dead because of sin. The sincere soul says, 'God knows that I have a thousand times tried a thorough and absolute mortification of every sin, and God has helped me to strive that it should no longer live in me. I have sometimes thought that I have come near to succeeding but I have always been disappointed. I am quite certain that while I am in this body, I shall never be without sin. It must be dead because of sin; sin's fibres and roots will never be plucked up, its nature will never be eliminated – the body can never be completely separated from it.' This is where we find the great mystery of the grave under the covenant of grace and by virtue of the death of Christ. What is this grave? Is it worms and corruption? No; it is God's refining-pot, his method of purification. There is no other way of separating sin and the body eternally but by consuming the body in the grave. A secret virtue issues from the death of Christ to the body of a believer laid in the grave that will eternally purify it, at its resurrection, from everything sinful.

I will not touch on what some have written of the state of the soul once the body is consumed in the grave, in that I do not wish to speak on anything that is questionable.

This, then, is the second reason: that all other attempts to eradicate sin have failed, having no success. They have brought me to be ashamed of myself, in the rebellion, darkness and unbelief of my nature. I will therefore be willing to part with my body. A believer in this position will then say, 'This is what God calls me to. Go, then, poor, mortal, sinful flesh, "You are dust, and to dust you shall return." I give you up to the doom of the Holy One, whose mouth has spoken it, that you must return to the dust. And there he will refine you and purify you, so that notwithstanding this separation, "my whole being rejoices; my flesh also dwells secure" (Psa. 16:9). For the time will come when "he will long for the work of his hands," when he "will call and you will answer him"' (Job 14:15, KJV). 'Do not be afraid to enter into darkness. Just as there is no sting in death, so there is no darkness in the grave, where you are going. It is merely a lying down in the hands of the great Refiner, who will purge, purify and restore you. Therefore, lie down in the dust in peace.'[2]

This is the second thing necessary for those who would die with their eyes open, cheerfully and comfortably, according to God's will: to be willing to leave this body to God's disposal, to be laid down in the dust. It is in this way it will come to see Christ, and in this way it will be finished with sin.

I will mention one other thing, very briefly, but it is the greatest thing that I would wish my own soul to apprehend. I pray that God would help me to do so. This is what I mean:

III. *Let us be careful not to be surprised by death.*

This is that specific wisdom to which God is calling our attention today. We do not know how soon we will be

[2] There is a similar strain of exhortation and reasoning, in which Christian faith and hope shine triumphant over the fears natural to men in the prospect of dissolution, in the author's preface to his 'Meditations on the Glory of Christ' (*Works*, vol. 1, p. 280). The reader will find the paragraph to which this note is appended on p. 283, wrought up and refined with the author's last touch and corrections, into a high degree of Christian eloquence.—W. H. Goold.

called upon by death. It may not come in an ordinary way, after a long sickness, giving us warning of its approach, nor wait until we have reached the age of a man 'threescore years and ten,' as the psalmist says. We may be surprised by it when we were not anticipating it. Anyone who has not learned this for himself from God's present dealings, in the world and in this congregation, will not believe even if someone were to return from the dead and tell him so. Let this, then, be fixed in your minds, that whatever your state and condition – some of you are strong, young and healthy, and some of us are old and feeble, on our way out of the world – every one of us could suddenly be surprised by death. Be careful, then, not to be surprised in a wrong frame. I hope that you all appreciate that there is great variety in the frames of believers. Sometimes they are in a good frame (grace is active and quick) they are ready to be impressed by the word and by warnings, delighting in holy thoughts. But at other times the world, tempta-tions, self-love, or the over-valuation of relationships may influence them so that they become very unfit and lifeless for the performance of duties with delight and vigour of spirit. They lose this zeal, though they keep up all their duties. I am sure that you can confirm this from your own experience.

You cannot maintain a lively, holy, living frame (though presenting an impression of it) except by an active medi-tation and constant view of things that are above. Many will tell you that when God has been pleased to keep their minds on thoughts of things above and to draw out their affections to cling to them, all has gone well with them; every prayer has life in it and every sermon and duty has pleasure and joy. Their hearts have rested and risen in peace. But when they have lost their view of spiritual things, all other things continue but with a kind of deadness about them. It is wise for us therefore to labour to maintain this spiritual view of eternal things by holy contemplation of them and by keeping them in our affections, otherwise death will surprise us. Whenever it comes, it will surprise you. But if we were to be in a dead frame, why would this messenger come at that time? Death is a messenger sent by God. He knocks at the door, but what does he come for? He comes to perfect your frame of mind and soul, that you may see heavenly things more clearly. He comes to untangle you from that deadness that burdens you, that darkness that surrounds you and to set you at perfect liberty to enjoy those things your soul loves. How then can your souls do anything other than to welcome this messenger?

Pray, therefore, that God will keep up your spirits by fresh supplies of his Spirit to maintain a view of heaven. You must do this by praying that God will give you fresh oil to increase light in your minds and understandings. Some can tell you from experience that, having made it their business with all their strength and study to live in that lively frame, yet at times they found that their light diminished so that it would not remain fixed upon heavenly things, nor affect the heart as it had once done. Their light would not continue to work, not until fresh supplies from the Holy Spirit gave life to it, and fresh oil enabled it to increase and to discern more clearly the beauty of spiritual and heavenly things.

In plain terms, I am speaking to dying men who do not know how soon they may die. May God advise my own heart that I should labour and watch so that death might not find me without a sight of eternal things! If it does – if our bellies cleave to the dust and our eyes turn to the ground; if we are filled with other things, and death approaches – do you think it will be an easy thing to gather in your minds and affections to agree to it and welcome it? You will not find it so. When David was in a good frame, he could say, 'You have redeemed me, O Lord, faithful God. O Lord, into your hand I commit my spirit.' 'I am willing to come and lay down this tabernacle and embrace this messenger.' But David relapsed from his good frame when his spirit cooled, and he complained of his case. Where now is the readiness and willingness of the good man to give up his spirit into the hands of God? 'O spare me, that I may recover strength' (Psa. 39:13, KJV). He is asking for a recovery, not of his physical strength, but of a better frame, one more fit to die in. And if death overcomes us in such a poor frame, the best of us will be found crying: 'O spare me a little, to recover strength.' 'O, the entanglements that have got hold of me by this and that temptation and distraction, by this coldness and decay! O Lord, spare me a little.' There is mercy with God for people in this state, but if it were the will of God, I would prefer that my cry would be, 'Lord, into your hands I commit my spirit; for you have redeemed me, O Lord God of truth.'

PURITAN PAPERBACKS

PURITAN PAPERBACKS

PURITAN 🕴 PAPERBACKS